The Mother's Manual

By Liu Yang

To My Daughter Ellen, With All My Love

Content Page

Appendices

Acknowledgement

I would like to show my gratitude to my colleagues whom I have worked with and learnt so much from over the past 20 years.

I want to thank my parents June and Min for doing their best to bring me up with all their love, their best intentions and any parenting knowledge that they had.

Most importantly, I want to relay my true appreciation to all the parents who have read the book and found it helpful in some way, and those who have sent me in their constructive feedback.

I would also like to give my sincere thanks to Susan Gault, my content and copy editor; Laura Helen Herbert and her team, my publisher, marketers, without whose support, the publishing of this book would not have been possible.

Introduction

"Give me a child until he is 7 and I will show you the man."

- Aristotle

The Mother's Manual is a practical handbook on parenting children from birth to 5 years old. There has been a great deal of research into the importance of bonding and nurturing children in the early years to benefit them for the rest of their lives. I have chosen the first 5 years because of my own clinical strength and expertise in this phase of children's development. This age division also fits in with the United Kingdom system where I currently practice. It is written for parents, parents to be and want-to-be parents.

In my 20 years of clinical practice as a health visitor, hypnotherapist and life coach, working with and understanding of people, families and their issues, plus extensive personal and professional development training, I have discovered a whole new world out there of knowledge and skills, which have helped me piece together this giant parenting puzzle.

I want to share ideas and processes about what I have learnt with you so that you can love, nurture, support and encourage your children using advanced communication skills to create the outcome you have planned, to offer your children the best start in life that they deserve, and to facilitate them on their journey of self-discovery.

We explore some common issues that crop up during those early critical years. The Manual provides practical tips on how to bring up a healthy and happy child, how to treat minor ailments, what to do if you are confronted with challenging behaviour, and skills and strategies that you can develop to help you be the best parent you can be.

I explain some strategies based on my best knowledge and understanding of emerging new scientific evidence over the past decade. I also include some interesting information in the appendix for you to browse at your leisure.

Whether you are planning to have children or are already pregnant, you can start practising some of the skills in this book and perfect them before your baby arrives, especially as new habits take time to establish.

How to use this book?

The Mother's Manual is designed for intervention, but more importantly prevention. It is aimed at promoting physical and emotional well-being for children and parents, helping them to develop good relationships and effective communication skills, and providing practical tips for behavioural management.

The content is designed to improve coping skills and problem solving for parents. Strategies to boost your confidence and parenting capacities are included. As well as focusing on the impact a baby may have on the couple's relationship, the book also shares an insight into how the couple's relationship can influence a child's life. Approaches to improve a couple's communication and promote understanding are included.

The book shows you some fundamental consideration and expectation of the reality when you are home with a new baby, the challenges that you face on your journey as a parent through your child's early life and his development at different ages and stages. I try to answer the most common questions that you may have along the way.

I've written this book in short sections so that you can read it from cover to cover, or one chapter at a time, or dip in and out as and when you need an answer to a specific question, issue or challenge. Use it as a reference book, a guide to check whether you are on the right track.

A word of caution

The principles in this book apply to healthy normal-term babies – babies who were born after 37 weeks of gestation – and babies without jaundice or any other conditions. Premature babies or children with more complex needs require specific care. Please seek your health visitor for specific advice.

I use stories where my parenting advice made a difference to parents' lives from my clinical experience in the hope that this will make it real for you with easy-to-follow steps to deal with an issue.

Any names used are made up to protect the person's identity and maintain confidentiality.

Although I appreciate very much all the input that fathers make in their children's lives, it's tedious to keep using mother, father, him and her. Therefore, I wrote this book as if I am talking to mothers. I chose to describe the parent as she and the child as he. So to simplify the issue, I use the assumption that there are two parents in the family. Same sex couples or single parents can easily adapt the principles in the book on their own or with another family member or friend to fulfil some of the father's role.

I wish your early parenting years to be as plain sailing as possible and as rewarding as they can be. They are such a few short few years, so make the most of this phase of your life and your child's life.

Chapter 1

Coming Home

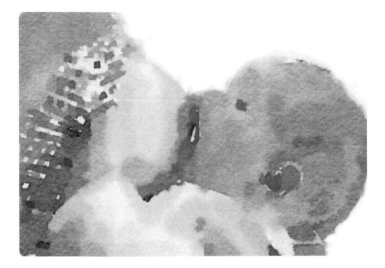

"*A new baby is like the beginning of all things - wonder, hope, a dream of possibilities.*"

- ***Eda J LeShan***

It's probably been quite a journey for you to get to this point, but now you are holding a baby in your arms. You have made it and it is time to appreciate what you have created.

For most women, this has meant months of planning your finances, your accommodation and your work; preparing your body with all the right vitamins, healthy food, quitting smoking or drinking; practising antenatal yoga, hypnobirth, some nappy changing skills on your friends' babies or your nieces and nephews, and patiently waiting to conceive and be pregnant for the whole 9 calendar months.

Now that your baby is home, it has probably just dawned on you that your life will never be the same again. Nothing can prepare you enough for the next days, weeks, months and years to come. A new beginning and a new family life are ahead of you, which will require new knowledge and skills in parenting to prepare you for this exciting ride.

Would you ever launch yourself into a new job at an executive level without any background knowledge and training? The answer probably is no. However, there is little comprehensive training available for the most important role in life called parenting. What are we thinking?

In this role, you hold the entire budget and make all the executive decisions. Your child's growth and development are a direct reflection of how you are performing. You don't need someone else like a boss to tell you off if anything goes wrong, you beat yourself up and torment yourself without end due to the strong bond and emotions between you and your child.

By now, as you are reading this book, I can assume that your baby probably has been checked and discharged by a paediatrician; you've had your midwife's visits in the first 10 days and your health visitor's visit between 10-14 days; your baby has also had his Vitamin K injection, a heel prick Guthrie test and a hearing test; his umbilical cord has dropped off; his jaundice is dissolving and the bloodshot in his eyes is dispersing.

Home alone

Your in-laws, relatives, friends and neighbours, and work colleagues have all visited you and your new baby. Your partner has taken his paternity leave and is back at work. Everything has settled down hopefully to a peaceful quietness. You are home alone with your baby, just the two of you. Now it's time to bond and begin to live your lives like you envisaged and planned.

Weeks 1 to 6

I won't reiterate all the important points that the health visitor will have made during her first visits to you about baby safety or the benefits of breast-feeding. Instead, I will focus on answering the four most common questions that parents have for this phase.

What shall you do and when:
1. Baby is not gaining sufficient weight according to the growth chart
2. Baby is not settling after a feed, causing tiredness, anxiety and frustration for both of you

3. You are suffering from sleeplessness that can cause low moods and relationship difficulties
4. You are feeling anxious about leaving the house on your own with your baby.

Feeding your baby

One of the major worries on many new mothers' minds is whether the baby is being fed enough milk. This is especially so for those who are breastfeeding their babies, as you can't see how much he has taken. All you know is that he wants to feed all the time, which may make you feel like you aren't producing enough milk to satisfy him. This is usually not the case.

Babies feed a lot. It is fairly normal for a baby to want a feed every 2-4 hours, assuming that the room temperature is right and he is a healthy baby without any ailments. Under special circumstances or if the weather is warm, he might feed more if he is hot and bothered. There isn't any justification for the baby to have water in the first 6 months before taking solids. Formula or breast milk is most adequate for him.

Before you breastfeed, prepare yourself and your environment so that you can relax and focus on your baby. It may not be so easy if this is your second or third baby and you have other young children to attend to. If you have a toddler, one of the simple tips is to get everything ready for your toddler. Settle the toddler with a drink, a game, some books, toys and snacks, and if you are potty training them, have a potty to hand in case they need to use it.

Get yourself into the mind-set that you are producing milk that is the right amount for your baby's needs. Always make sure that you have eaten and drunk water yourself before breastfeeding, because it is hard for your body to produce milk when it is dehydrated.

When you are breastfeeding, you must first ensure that your baby has a **good latch** by ensuring he takes a large mouthful of your breast, particularly the areola, and your breast is comfortable when he sucks. If you can hear your baby swallowing after 2-3 sucks, it means he is getting milk from his efforts. If the baby's latch is poor, you will feel pain and your baby will suffer from wind, because of swallowing air through the gap.

One mother really wants me to emphasise the importance of a good latch from day one and every time thereafter. She says that once the nipple is sore or broken down, it is very difficult to heal due to the frequency of the feeds. She was feeding 18 times a day with a newborn who was born with two teeth. She persevered with the support from professionals and later settled down to 10 feeds a day when the baby was a month old. The result is really worth it when you come through from the other end.

Poor latch, such as only sucking the tip of the nipple, could flatten the milk ducts with a result like sucking a flat straw. If latch is poor, you can sometimes see light-coloured pinch marks on the side of the nipple made by your baby gnawing on the nipple alone. Apart from poor latch, this can also be a result of tongue-tie, which you will need to get professional help for. He will get tired and frustrated because very little milk is coming out of the flattened milk duct despite a lot of hard sucking. He may give up and fall asleep.

Feeding by sucking is a new skill for your baby, which he has to learn fast. Remember, he hasn't done it before. So be patient with him and with yourself, because this is a whole new experience for both of you. Offer him plenty of opportunities to practise finding the nipple, which is best done at home where you are most relaxed, with skin-to-skin contact and when he is not so hungry. Stroke him gently to demonstrate encouragement and reassurance.

If you are having difficulties, take advice from professionals and friends, and then think about what works for you, and once clear, just keep going. If your baby is putting on weight steadily, whatever you are doing is fine because it is working. Give yourself a high five if there is no one else around to pat you on the back.

When your baby finishes his feed, which takes between 30 to 60 minutes for a newborn, he might want to stay on the breast and do little nibbling soothing sucks, which should be encouraged. Women sometimes mistake this phenomenon as indicating that they don't have enough milk. In fact, the more he sucks, the more signals are being sent to your brain to produce more milk. It is a demand-supply relationship. He is growing daily. By continuously sucking on the breast, even if it feels like he is using you as a human dummy after a feed, he is actually sending a request to your brain for more milk to be produced for the next feed. You will produce more milk as he gets bigger.

When your baby has fed enough, he will come off the breast on his own and feel content. Try to offer him the second breast, because the milk composition is different between the watery foremilk and the rich and creamy hindmilk. He might just fancy some lighter milk to finish off his feed. It also gives your other breast a chance to be stimulated. It is always a good sign if your baby has lots of wet and pooey nappies in the early days to indicate that he is feeding sufficiently.

Although scientists suggest that a newborn will need around 150-200 mls of milk per kilogram of weight in any 24-hour period during the first 6 months, it is not easy to guess how much your baby has taken in from the breasts. Some mothers express milk so that they can measure the quantity and then bottle-feed the breast milk to their baby. In my opinion, this could jeopardise the baby's ability to breastfeed as the sucking techniques needed for sucking a breast and sucking a bottle are so different. Sucking a bottle is possibly easier, with less effort needed by your baby. If you feel the need to express, I would suggest doing this when breastfeeding is established, usually after a few weeks. If your breast is very sore, this is usually due to poor latching on. Get support from your health visitor who can offer or direct you to the right support you need.

If you need to top up the baby with formula or by choice if you prefer it, there is usually a guide amount stated on the tin. It is only a guide. So if in doubt, simply have your baby weighed in a clinic to ensure that he is on track and get the reassurance from the staff there.

Feeding pattern

There is usually no set feeding pattern in the early days. Once you have a realistic expectation, you can accept the situation more easily and readily. And I promise you, your child will eventually settle into a feeding pattern after a couple of months, which will give you some time to yourself in between the feeds.

Make the most of this comparatively short phase in your child's life by developing a bond through skin-to-skin contact, enjoying your time together day and night, cluster feeding like mad on and off the breast non-stop for an hour or two, or dream feeding when he is half-asleep without waking him up fully. Have a bite to eat by having cooked finger food around the house where it is easy to grab and catch a nap when you can. Before you know it, your child will be at that age when you can start training him into a routine that you want.

Temperature control

Newborns grow fast, changing and developing on a daily basis. Their brain and many other organs in the body aren't fully functional at birth. One of the things that you have to help your newborn with is regulating his temperature by setting a correct room temperature at around 19 degrees Celsius and putting a vest and a baby grow on him, and covering him with 2 layers of cotton cellular baby blanket. His hair follicles are not fully formed, so that he can get very warm and uncomfortable quickly, and become thirsty as a result of being too warm and becoming dehydrated. When he is in the ultimate room temperature with the right amount of cover, he will want to feed only when he's hungry. It's equally dangerous for him to get too cold as well as too hot. In this modern day, when probably all homes with a new baby have central heating, over-heating is a more common problem.

Instead of buying all kinds of expensive gadgets to check his body temperature, you can simply check with your nice and warm hands. Put your warm hand on the back of his neck or on the skin of his chest or tummy, ask yourself whether his body is a lot warmer than your hand. You have got the temperature right for him if you feel both your temperatures are pretty much the same around 36.5 degrees Celsius. We humans are mammals so that we are able to maintain our body temperature at a consistent level at around 36.5 degrees Celsius as a full-grown healthy adult. That's what you are aiming for. Your hand is the most reliable gadget.

Other safety aspects of having a newborn

Apart from temperature control, you need to be aware of the harmful effect of secondary smoking and the increased risk of cot death with smokers in the household. Make sure that there is nobody smoking around the baby. There isn't a safe period for how long you should wait after smoking before picking up your baby, but certainly the longer the better. Some people try to wash their hands, one dad even told me that he has a shower after his cigarette, but it is in your lungs and in your breath. So if you are serious about doing the best for your baby and giving up smoking, I would suggest getting help from your family doctor.

The risk of co-sleeping has been controversial. Some research suggests that it is okay to do it if you are not tired. I always challenge that by asking which new parents are not tired. I have not come across one in 20 years. By all means have as much skin-to-skin contact as possible in bed when you are fully awake. But remember, the minute you feel sleepy, put the baby down in a safe place like his cot before you catch a nap.

You should always place your baby to sleep on his back and cover him with a blanket, when necessary depending on temperature, by loosely tucking the blanket under his armpits, so that his arms are free. Babies tend to startle easily, and this will prevent him from struggling and pulling the blanket over his face, causing breathing difficulties.

Some mothers still practise swaddling. This is a traditional practice that has now been shown to cause hip dislocation in cases where the baby is very tightly bound. I have also seen a risk of suffocation when babies kick their swaddling blanket loose so that it shifts all the way to the top near their mouth and nose. So simply tuck the blanket or muslin sheet under your baby's armpits, when used.

Last but not least, all mothers with more than one child understand the importance of constant supervision. This applies to your family pets too. I mean constant supervision, because accidents can occur in a split second. If you have to leave the room to do something else, take the toddler who needs supervision most because they can get into danger just by exploring the world around them.

Gaining weight

You know that your baby is feeding well when he has regained his birth weight at around day 10-14. Occasionally, I see a baby who takes longer than 3 weeks to regain his birth weight. In a couple of very rare cases, the baby didn't regain birth weight for six weeks due to pathological reasons. If your baby hasn't regained his birth weight by 3 weeks, you should talk to your health visitor about feeding and to your family doctor (GP) just in case there are any underlying conditions that are preventing him from gaining weight. The most common ones are gastric reflux, infections and allergies. In more rare cases, the baby might have a heart condition that wasn't picked up at birth.

Babies on average put on a pound every 2 weeks for the first 4 months, and then a pound a month until the age of one. This is only a guide. The best way to know whether your baby is growing well is to have him weighed in a baby clinic near you. Ask your family doctor if you are not sure where the clinic is.

For formula-fed babies, you need to increase the amount of milk you give your baby gradually according to his appetite. What it says on the tin is only guidance. Each baby has his own metabolic rate like us, so listen to your baby.

Unsettled baby

Now your baby has been gaining steady weight. You have just accomplished a massive task. Give yourself a pat on the back. Now you begin to wonder why you have to carry him all the time and why he cries. Crying is the only way that he can communicate with you in the first few weeks. Babies cry for a reason, although the reason might not be apparent. It's up to you to find out what's going on. Become a mind reader.

I always ask couples how long it takes for them to get to know each other. It takes time to get to know your baby too. If you listen carefully, the tone of crying is different depending on whether your baby is hungry, bored, has a dirty nappy or is in discomfort. How you respond to his crying will also influence how he will cry the next time he wants something. You are communicating with each other, training each other and developing your own unique relationship pattern.

It is not always straightforward to understand what your child needs. I normally suggest that parents write a list of the things that they can do to soothe their baby, e.g. feeding, cuddling, entertaining, removing clothes, putting on an extra layer of blanket, going out in the fresh air, taking them for a drive in the car, etc. I have known mothers to put their unsettled baby in the car and drive around at 3am in the morning to try to settle him (something about the motion of the drive seems to soothe some babies), while others will be soothed by the sound of the hoover or a hair dryer.

The more you pay attention to the sound of your baby's crying, the easier it will be to guess what he needs and how to comfort him. It is a process of trial and error. You will get there in the end. The key is to remain calm, because when you are stressed, your baby will sense your anxiety, and become more unsettled and cry more. So if you feel that you have tried everything and he is still crying, let someone else who is calm and relaxed have a go at cuddling him to see whether he will settle down. If he cries non-stop regardless of what you do, he may be in pain, so I would take him to be checked over by a doctor.

Is it wind or acid reflux?

As a general rule of thumb, babies with gastric reflux tend to cry and arch their backs once the feeding starts, because the stomach begins to produce acid for digesting the protein in the milk. On the other hand, a windy baby tends to feel the discomfort after he has been fed, often making cycling motions with his legs like he is riding a bike.

Another common reason why babies become unsettled is from overheating. I know it all too well, being from a Chinese background. In the Chinese culture, the baby is supposed to be wrapped up well even in the summer. My daughter developed pussy heat bumps all over her head due to overheating, as she was born in July and didn't need the amount of wrapping up I gave her.

Most parents understand that they must keep the baby warm, otherwise they develop hypothermia. However, overheating is equally dangerous, because your baby could develop a fever. The common causes of overheating are a high room temperature with too many layers covering the baby. So bear this in mind and use your warm hand to feel the skin on the back of his neck or his tummy to gauge his temperature. If he is so much warmer than your hand, strip off a couple of layers.

I visited a baby in one of the hottest British summers. I saw that his mum had wrapped the baby in layers of blankets by swaddling the baby, while the room temperature was 24 degrees Celsius. I suggested to her that this might be too much for the baby in such hot weather since the baby was snacking often on the breast, which can be a sign of feeding for thirst. She was receptive to my advice and unwrapped the baby during my visit. However, the following day, I received an A+E notification to say that the baby had ended up in hospital overnight. They thought the baby, who had a spiking temperature, had a serious infection. All clinical investigations produced normal results. I wouldn't be surprised if the baby had heatstroke.

There may be other reasons causing your baby to be unsettled. Please refer to Chapter five.

Baby blues or post-natal depression

During the early days of coming home with a new baby, parents normally experience tiredness due to interrupted sleep caused by frequent feeds and attendance to the baby's needs. For mothers, the fact that your hormone level is coming down can cause tearfulness in the early days. This is normally called the 'baby blues'.

Remember to eat as well. During my antenatal classes, women used to laugh when I told them to remember to eat after giving birth. They thought I was joking because they were eating a lot more frequently during their pregnancy. They only found out later after giving birth that they had been rushing around since 6am and when I visited them around lunchtime, they were yet to have eaten breakfast or even taken sips of water. So look after number one. You need to be fit and healthy, as there is nobody else as well attuned to your baby's needs as you, his mother.

When your needs are not met, your body won't sustain peak performance. So remember to eat and have healthy finger food or snacks available at all times. You will be amazed how you soon learn to do most things with one hand, for example, eating and drinking when you are feeding the baby, and sleeping as soon as he goes down.

You should also continue with a healthy balanced diet plus the multivitamins you were taking during pregnancy, especially if you are breastfeeding, because your baby gets his share through your breast milk. However, a new recommendation is that breastfed babies should be given a Vitamin D supplement regardless whether or not their mothers are taking Vitamin D supplement. Babies who are formula-fed or mix-fed (a combination of breast milk and formula) who take at least 500 millilitres of formula in a 24-hour period don't require a Vitamin D supplement because they will get sufficient Vitamin D from the formula.

If this is your first baby, try to have a rest or a nap when your baby sleeps. After a good feed, he could sleep up to 5 hours at a stretch in any 24 hours. If you are not good at sleeping during the day, then you will need to follow the guidance on getting your baby into a routine sooner which will be discussed in a later chapter. Make the most of whatever time you have the first time round. You won't be so lucky with your second child when you have a toddler running around in the house.

Feeling anxious about going out with your baby on your own

Going out and getting fresh air is beneficial because babies love fresh air and they tend to settle well with motion. Even if you are at home, make sure the windows are slightly open as long as the baby is not in the draft. By taking in fresh air and sunlight, apart from getting the very much needed Vitamin D production by the skin, the effect on the production of the sleep hormone melatonin in the body helps the baby establish a natural rhythm that can enhance his regular awake and sleep cycle, so that he will be awake more during the day and sleep at night.

It used to be okay for you to do things on the spur of the moment when you were on your own or with your partner who's happy to follow your style. However, a baby doesn't quite get it at the beginning and has a mind of his own. When he is hungry, he wants to be fed. When he doesn't get what he wants, he cries to make his wish known. When his nappy is dirty, he wants to be changed immediately even if you are just about to walk out of the door.

Now it requires some organisational skills even if you were not organised before. Plan ahead and give yourself plenty of time before you meet any friends, join any groups or go to the clinic. This will help to reduce your stress levels and help you feel relaxed and more in control.

I also suggest to mothers to ask their partners or parents to accompany them when they go out for the few first times. It is important that you learn to manage on your own, but it is reassuring to know that you have someone to call upon if you need to on your first ventures outside your home with your new baby. I have seen women manage to go out confidently after a couple of accompanied rounds.

Ask for help

Asking for help may not come as naturally for some people. I also recommend getting as much help as you can. It is important to organise your visitors' visiting times and activities. Instead of letting well-wishing people do what they feel necessary, give them clear instructions about what you would like them to help you with. You will find that by doing so everyone is happy, because they have the satisfaction of helping you and you have the joy of getting the help when you need it. You simply need to communicate clearly.

If you have time, you can also cook a batch of food to leave in the freezer, so that you can quickly defrost it, heat it up and eat it. There are also some good-quality ready meals, which you can stock up on, so you can focus more on rest and feeding the baby.

I have come across more community groups helping their families with newborns by having volunteers provide a meal for the family each day for the first 30 days after their baby's birth. Get all the support you need, because you can do with it now. You can always pay those people back in other ways in the future. That's what being part of a community is about.

Chapter 2

Love and Connection

"You will never find time for anything. If you want time, you must make it."

- Charles Buxton

The transition to parenthood is generally considered to be one of the most challenging events in life and for a relationship. Some evidence suggests that how a couple manages the arrival of their first child is a good indicator of how long their relationship will continue.

Having a baby certainly causes huge changes in relationships with your partner, extended family, your friends and, more importantly, to your own life as you move into parenthood.

Having young children often causes a strain on a couple's relationship for a number of reasons. Lack of sleep caused by frequent feeding of the baby and the amount of time spent settling him seem to take over your life and leave no time for anything else. You may find it more difficult to go out with your partner or friends to enjoy the things that you used to do. You feel somewhat cut off from your old life – the life you knew.

Me time

You get a surge of Oxytocin in your body naturally after birth and during breastfeeding, which plays a pivotal role in bonding and attachment in the first 4-6 weeks while the "maternal instinct" kicks in. Oxytocin is a powerful hormone. The level in our body goes up when we kiss or hug or have a sexual relationship with a loved one. You now instinctively want what is best for your baby by feeding him, rocking him, bathing him, patting him. You become a selfless being for him, perhaps forgetting to eat or drink, with a reduced sensation of pain and being totally devoted to developing an exclusive relationship between the two of you. Sometimes, this can trigger your motherly defensive nature and you can become more critical towards your partner or other helpers if they don't appear to care for your baby to your standards and intensity.

Being a parent, you often rush around attending to your baby's needs and everyone else's. It is very nice and good if you have lots of people around you serving your needs. It is equally fine if you are on your own, you simply need to remember the importance of looking after number one. The truth is once you have children, your whole focus turns toward them. You do not just neglect your own needs but even the needs of your partner and friends.

"Me time" when you relax and do something pleasurable just for you, whether it is a nice bath by candlelight or a gentle stroll along a river canal, is essential for your long-term health and well-being. When you are relaxed, everyone else is relaxed around you. World-renowned family therapist Cloe Madanes always says "happy mother, happy home".

Having "me time" is far from being selfish, it is indispensable. You need to meet your own basic needs first to survive, and once you love yourself first and meet your own needs, then you will be able to give unconditional love to others. Your partner, your children, your friends and relatives, even your neighbours and your co-workers will become happy by feeling your happiness and upbeat energy. You are like a vase with water. There is nothing to flow out of your vase if you are empty.

You will have nothing to give – experiencing a "burn out" – if you are just giving without receiving. So put your feet up and enjoy life on a regular basis. Only by meeting your needs will you feel at peace with yourself and others. Your baby will be calmer when you are happy because he will sense your state, your energy and your vibration. Haven't you noticed that your child seems to play up more when you are tired or after a tough day?

I normally visit families in the late morning to give them a chance of a good lie-in and time to get ready for their day. Many have actually been up since the crack of dawn when their baby woke up, and have done their house chores like laundry and cleaning, and before they knew it, it was noon and they hadn't even had any breakfast or a sip of water.

I remember the days when I used to run antenatal classes. Women often laughed when I told them to remember to eat and drink after the baby is born. The above story is not uncommon. So remember to eat and drink by having a glass of water on the table and a bowl of fruit handy to remind you.

According to human needs psychologists, we all have six Human Needs, which drive our behaviour. They are certainty, variety, significance, love and connection, growth and contribution. We only feel truly fulfilled once all of these needs are met.

We do try to find our own ways to meet these needs knowingly or unknowingly on a daily basis. These fundamental human needs are the drive of our behaviour. These needs of yours or your partner's have to be met one way or another. Most people have these met subconsciously, which explains sometimes why you don't understand why you have done certain things when reflecting on it afterwards. For instance, if your partner really values love and connection as his top value and his needs can't be met at home, he will have to have them met elsewhere. This doesn't mean that he is going to have an affair with a woman; he may have an affair with his work or his golf.

Same for you, if you don't have your needs met by your partner because he is busy with work, his colleagues, his meetings, his travel and his hobbies, then you would, for instance, seek love and connection elsewhere such as from your children, your siblings, your friends and your family. You might experience a passionless relationship even though you love each other very much. However, at the end of the day, only couples who can meet each other's needs feel love, joy, passion and liveliness.

There are different ways of meeting these needs in beneficial ways or in destructive ways such as seeking solace in drugs and alcohol. If you have a behaviour that you don't like, think of what need it is meeting: does it make you feel safe and secure, does it give you a bit of spice in life, does it make you feel connected or important? Then find constructive alternatives such as open communication with honesty, sharing your thoughts and feelings, making a date with your partner, doing some fun things together like before you had children, enjoying regular family dinner times, etc. to meet those needs.

Us time

Romance and love-making normally take a backstage when you have just welcomed your new baby home. Both of you are totally focusing on this new arrival and both are exhausted after a huge emotional upheaval during the delivery and many sleepless nights. Some women experience pain from wounds or sutures after the delivery. Women often tell me "that's the last thing on their mind" when I talk to them about contraception during my visit after the baby is born. Nonetheless, there are true stories in my experience of women who discovered they were pregnant again soon after their delivery.

Sexual intercourse can be uncomfortable soon after the childbirth. There isn't a right time to resume your sex life. It is when you feel ready and feel right. A little lubricant might help with the penetration and contraception should be sought if you haven't planned to have another baby in 10 months.

Ten per cent of women suffer from postnatal depression – a hormonal imbalance – in the first year after birth, which can be exacerbated by social and economic circumstances. If you feel lack of interest in yourself, your baby or anything else, you have a poor appetite or sleep poorly (even when your baby and everyone else is asleep), experience tearful moments, mood swings or overwhelming anxiety, you should seek support from professionals.

Each case is different. Talk to your health visitor or doctor for a further assessment if you have any doubt. There is commonly a check of yourself and your baby by your family doctor between 6-8 weeks after you deliver your baby. Post-natal depression can be identified around this time or at a later date, at around a year after the birth, when you need to go back to work and experience separation anxiety from your baby.

How your partner can help?

Open communication is the key. Talk things through, such as how you feel if he says something that upsets you and how you would prefer him to say it. Teach him and train him. It is only fair if you give him a chance and opportunity to learn. Ask your partner to spend time devoted to listening to you if he doesn't already. Ask to be cuddled or held after a bad night, because men don't always get exactly what you want or need. When they don't want to get a foot wrong, sometimes they do nothing. So ask him and you shall receive.

The secret to achieving the ultimate relationship is to be able to sense each other's needs with the intention to tune in to each other's energy and frequency just like you do with your baby. You were not sure exactly what your baby needed at the beginning, but as time goes on, you get it right over and over again. You develop a rapport, an understanding of his needs once you open your heart and do your best to understand him.

It becomes easy after some practice. Just spend quiet time together, looking into each other's eyes with love. This will begin the synchronisation of your breathing, your heart rate, your feelings and your thinking. Remember those moments when you said "you have read my mind!"

By being present for each other, it's like you intentionally tune into each other's radio stations, you pick up each other's broadcasting signals simply by having a pure intention to understand each other. You will get why your partner feels the way they feel and what made them do what they did, you will get the answers you seek, and vice versa.

Catch yourself when you are off track such as being critical or snappy, bring yourself back to your heart, show your desire for love, show vulnerability, ask yourself what's important, what outcome you want to achieve and start again. The more you do it this way, the easier it gets.

Now it is always a good time to improve your relationship, write a new chapter, make history, make a new decision, take a new direction in life, take action, make new choices, to experience love, to connect, to forgive and to feel compassion. By communicating openly and clearly about what you want, you offer your partner an opportunity to meet your needs or make up if they have made mistakes.

It helps to say "I am sorry" if you realise that you have done wrong, followed by "What can I do to make it right?". If you want to continue working on this relationship to make it grow, there is always a way. There are always things that you can do to correct the mistakes of the past and start afresh.

"There is no love without forgiveness, and there is no forgiveness without love."
- Bryant H. McGill

Communication styles

Remember that there are fundamental differences between men and women when it comes to how they think and express their thoughts. I understand that each person is a unique individual and has their own personal communication style. But there are some general truths about the sexes.

Men tend to prefer a more direct communication style; they like to solve problems rather than just talk about them. They like to do things and when there isn't anything they can do to help you, they get frustrated. Women are more indirect in their communication styles and imply things more often with subtle words or lifted eyebrows or a look, tone of voice or body gesture. They like to share their thoughts and feelings. Women sometimes just want someone to listen to them. We humans are by nature social animals.

Men aren't usually quick to pick up or interpret those ambiguous cues. When they have tried a couple of times to help you "get things right" by their way of understanding, but without your appreciation, they gradually resign themselves and end up not really being present or listening to you, which causes you more frustration and even a loss of that connection. You might communicate less and allow the pressure cooker to build up and eventually erupt, leaving devastating debris.

Eliminate words like "can't, won't, don't". So be clear and direct about what you want and why you want it from the depth of your heart. Set yourself to communicate it simply and directly to your partner. Men apparently genuinely want to make their women happy believe or not. You can carry out your own survey yourself. They only resign when they can't figure out a way to make that happen. Being grateful and expressing your gratitude towards your man is only going to incentivise him to do more of what you want.

Do you recall a moment when you were so tired, the baby was crying all night and all day, you were thinking about taking him to see a doctor, and when your partner suggested that you get a takeaway for dinner asking what you'd like to have, you snapped at him, "can't you just order it. Don't you know what I like after all these years?" Now, do you remember another time when you were absolutely in a good mood, your partner had done something clumsy like spilling wine on the carpet or putting something in the wrong place, and you just said "it's ok" with a smile on your face saying "where would you be without me".

How we react and respond to a situation is largely dependent on our own emotional state – what we think and how we feel. So it is necessary to master our own emotions and tame our thoughts. Here are some simple suggestions that you can try.

How to lift your mood and change your emotional state

You can lift your mood into a calmer emotional state by:

- Listening to a favourite piece of music
- Doing a dance move
- Walking up and down the stairs for 5 minutes

- Having a nice bath while baby sits in the bouncy chair watching you
- Sitting or standing quietly while inhaling a breath of fresh air in the garden for 2 minutes
- Inviting your best friend over for a cup of tea or talking to them on the phone for 5 minutes
- Asking your partner to give you a back rub
- Watching a film or funny clips on YouTube
- Putting the baby in the pram and going out for a walk or a drive. I know mothers have done the drive in the middle of the night
- Taking your baby to a baby clinic and talking to the professionals there
- Meeting other mothers in your post-natal group

One of the mothers I visited told me that she uses the 1-minute rule. She just gives herself the time to stay quiet (you can always retreat to the bathroom for some space) and empty her mind for a minute if she feels anxiety or a low mood creeping in.

So whatever works for you, I would love to hear about it from you.

When you are dealing with a situation in a calmer state, you speak more coherently, clearly and explain yourself more lucidly.

You can see how your physical, mental and emotional well-being is pivotally important to yourself and everyone around you. You will naturally be calmer and happier if you are in a joyful mood once your needs are met. So look after number one.

How good life is, is largely dependent upon your communication skills, including verbal and non-verbal. Most problems occur when others don't understand you and they don't know what you need, and just do whatever they think best is for you and assume that's what you need. The better you communicate, the easier it is for others to understand your needs and serve you. People are trying to be helpful especially those who are around you and love you.

Ask a friend or relative or pay a babysitter so you and your partner can have time together, even if it's just for a walk in the park. Share the housework with some ground rules so you can have more time enjoying life. Family therapist Cloe Madanes says: "It's cheaper to have a babysitter than a divorce lawyer."

A solid couple relationship has a pivotal importance in your parenting role. When you two fight, your children feel they have to get involved and take a side, so they are torn between you. Your united front shows your children the strength, leadership and union of your relationship as a couple and, most important of all, it provides a role model for them to follow in their relationships in the future. Good relationships will extend to your neighbours, school friends, relatives and your in-laws once you are happy in yourself.

Plan a date

Have regular dates with your partner. It is good to go out once a week, especially during this post-natal period. This time could give you an opportunity to air things out, share joy or differences, find solutions, figure out your emotional triggers and how to avoid them, and repair any misunderstandings, stating clearly how you would like things to happen and planning for action in a timely fashion. This could be some of the best time that you spend that saves your relationship.

Manage extended family

When two people meet, they create a new dimension that has its rules, standards, goals and dreams. Now things have changed again since the arrival of your baby. When a third party — a brand new baby — is introduced, he comes with his own agenda and can set things for a spin. Your priority has now changed, possibly together with competing values, rules and standards due to the natural variations between you and your partner.

This is why you need to talk about how you would like to bring up your children, including passing on your values, standards and discipline, etc., before you have a baby, preferably during courtship if relevant. Clear the air as soon as possible to save arguments later, such as deciding on principles like whether you want to bring your baby up eating meat or being a vegetarian. Be flexible and find a middle ground.

Now, the dynamic in the family system has changed, so have your relationship structures. What I want to emphasise here is to maintain that hierarchy – you and your partner are the leaders of your family-ship together. Everyone else, including your parents and children, need to respect the decisions made by each of you.

It is important to keep a united front when you are with others. You are a unit as a couple. You can resolve anything between you if you have a loving intention to make the relationship work and each other happy. With any external interference with its own agenda and priority, it's going to create some turbulence. Things can be tipped out of balance.

Children can easily get in the crack if there is one between you and your partner. If your child tells you that daddy says it is okay when you don't think he should have done so, simply reply "let me discuss it with daddy first". Remember the time when you were on a netball team, you never blamed your teammate if she did something wrong, you simply told her what she should be doing next time in a similar situation.

You are a team, a family unit. You are the team leaders. You both are examples and role models for your children. How would you want them to be? Then demonstrate that through your joint effort and actions. If you have a consistent united front, demonstrate leadership and strength, your children will soon follow suit and be on track to where you want them to be. Your relationship style will also influence your children's future choice of partner and how they parent their children when the time comes.

Chapter 3

Establishing a Routine

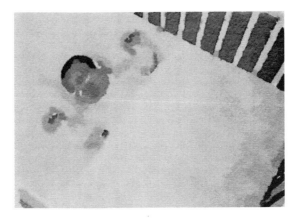

"My message is simple: Take control of your life"

- Charles Barkley

You have now managed to survive with little sleep, and feed the baby on demand for the past 2 months, that's 8 weeks, 56 days. You have survived one of the first major challenges in a new parent's life. Well done and congratulations. The toughest time without sleep is over. It is now time to claim your life back. Now it's time to consider establishing a routine for your baby.

The reason for this timing at 8 weeks is that newborns do not have enough melatonin – a hormone produced by the pineal gland in the brain. It helps control sleep and awake cycles – the circadian biological clock that we normally call the body clock.

You can train your baby to sleep at night at a later time of course. You need to do it at a time that you think is right – when you feel that he is ready. Each baby is different. I do believe in the mother's instinct. You know your baby better than anyone else, so follow your instinct. The earliest time to naturally consider a routine is around 2 months of age if this is your first baby.

You might have to introduce some sort of routine earlier if this is your second or third child, as your older children will have their routines, such as nursery or school, activities, etc. It is important to keep their routine going whenever you can, especially if a new sibling in their lives has already caused some disruption.

I would advise establishing a routine as soon as you are ready. The earlier you start, the easier it is. I have helped parents to train their over 3-year-old children to sleep in their own beds. That's a completely different ballgame compared with training a baby to sleep in his cot because toddlers can walk and get into your room and your bed. So start as soon as you are ready. The latest time for you to start a routine should be at 6 months ideally. The older your baby gets, the cleverer and more aware he is, and the habit of seeing you at night will take more effort to break.

Planning your routine

Routines differ from family to family. You simply need to establish a routine that works for you. It is good to do a bit of planning. Start by keeping a diary for 7 days and writing down what time your baby naturally feeds, is awake or sleeps.

You also need to work out what you would like to happen, for example, a tea break at 3 pm with a friend? Yes, that kind of a plan. Once you know what you want to do, then you can look at what your baby is doing, and gradually move towards a perfect fit.

Each family has its own routine. It is whatever works for you. Some prefer for the baby go to sleep at 6 pm and get up 6 am. I visited the owner of a French restaurant who doesn't want their baby to sleep until midnight so that they can sleep until midday. You want to establish a routine that works for you and your family.

A routine with your first baby can also be different from that with your second or subsequent children. When you have a toddler running around, you won't be able to sleep even when you want to because you need to supervise the older one. So make the most of it, the first time round.

Generally speaking, it takes on average a few days to get a baby into a routine if you try to do the same thing at the same time during the training period. The earlier you start, usually the easier it is, such as soon as from 2 months onwards. Babies are very intelligent and will pick up a consistent message quickly.

Once you have got your baby into a routine, you should stick to the new timetable for a couple of months or so to condition his body for it to become a habit and for the Circadian Rhythm to kick in. This is to condition the baby's brain to make an association between the sleep cues and the sequence meaning sleep time. After that, the baby will simply drop off to sleep at the time that you have scheduled within minutes, thanks to his body clock.

Being consistent is the key. Otherwise your baby will get confused if one minute he can sleep in your bed and the next he's expected to sleep in his own cot. By being consistent, your baby will get a consistent message loud and clear, so that he will get it sooner.

It is critical to your success that you and your partner are consistent, and that you both commit to the same technique. Anything else can cause confusion to the baby, and ultimately interfere and prolong the process.

Planning by talking to your partner or other people in the household to get their support and agreement is critical to your success. The hardest thing is when you are trying to train your baby to sleep and your partner asks you to pick the baby up and sort him out due to the disturbance from his crying. It will be easier for you and the baby if you have a united front and are consistent with your approach.

You need to support each other in time of need, especially when the baby is crying so that you can quickly decide what to do.

Lights on or off

Studies have shown that the light emitted by screens such as TV, computer, phone, etc., known as the blue light, suppresses melatonin levels, making it more difficult to fall asleep.

Red lights are said to be the least likely to suppress melatonin levels according to scientists. This makes a red light a perfect option for bed lights and nightlights.

These days you can purchase a light bulb from large home stores that automatically changes colours. I have had parents reporting that red light helps their babies to sleep, as the research has suggested.

Change of routine

Any change of routine could interfere with your baby's routine and throw it temporarily out of sync. For instance, routine sometimes goes out of the window when you are on holiday so that you have to re-establish the routine again when you get home. Similarly, you might have to start again if your child is poorly, you have visitors staying over, after he has had an immunisation, etc. However, re-establishing a routine should be a lot quicker the next time around.

Flexibility during the day

I always suggest trying to be more flexible during the day by feeding your baby on demand so that he is fuller and sleeps with longer feeding intervals during the night. You can intentionally prolong the intervals between feeds at night little by little by changing his nappy, or giving him a gentle cuddle and chatting to him in order to delay feeding him for say 15 minutes at a time for the next few days. If you do the same every night, he will get used to the new timing, and you can delay another 15 minutes every few days thereafter. You eventually will get an interval between feeds of up to 5 hours in one stretch. He would not need a night feed when he is 6 months old. However, if you stick to a routine too rigidly during the day, he may not get enough feeds and may wake up often during the night to catch up on his feeds.

How much sleep does a baby need?

The amount of sleep a baby needs varies just like in adults. Newborn babies tend to sleep around 16-18 hours. This gradually reduces as they get older and the intervals between feeds get longer, especially at night. Most babies under the age of 6 months will still require one night feed, although some will sleep through the night.

Creating sleep cues

Melatonin levels begin to increase at least an hour before a person goes to sleep, so plan when you want your baby to fall asleep and carry out the preparation that is essential, such as turning all electronic gadgets off, adjusting to low light and putting on some soft music a couple of hours beforehand. This helps to regulate the melatonin secretion.

You may not have an hour's preparation time during the day, so try to continue with a simple version of cues for sleep as well if you want, including feeding, changing, reading a story and kissing good-night. In terms of background noise, some babies love it and some don't. You have to find out what your baby prefers and adjust accordingly.

In order to have a good sleep, both adults and children need some healthy exercise and fresh air during the daytime.

You probably already have learnt the sound that your baby makes before he wants to sleep such as soft grunts and cries, rubbing the eyes, yawning, etc. Now it's time for the sleep cues.

So the sleep routine should start with quiet time before bedtime such as reading stories with a quiet and calm tone of voice or listening to some soft music. Please ensure that you turn off all gadgets because the blue light emanating from the screens can interfere with the sleep hormone's production.

Plan ahead. Give yourself an hour to carry out the bedtime cues before you want him to be asleep. You can begin with washing/bathing in a relatively calm manner because too much excitement could result in nightmares and because the brain is still active, it also makes it harder for him to settle. When your child is old enough, make sure that you brush his teeth as soon as possible after his last feed. Then put him in his cot when he is sleepy but has not yet completely fallen asleep. If he manages to fall asleep on his own in his cot, when he wakes up at night, which he will do, he will learn to get himself back to sleep again by himself.

Quiet and monotonous reading of a story or singing a lullaby is a good part of the settling routine. Then kiss your child good night, dim the light and leave the room. You can leave the door open slightly with the hallway light on if he prefers.

Over the years, I have found that babies seem to feel more secure when they can hear some of the household noises, reassuring them that there are people around. Some low light from the corridor through a slightly opened door will be adequate.

Remember each baby is unique. If you have found that your baby loves pitch black with total silence, then so be it. Practise what works for you. The only drawback might be later when he might find it difficult to sleep anywhere else rather than his own home in his own bed at that exact environment. So having an imperfect environment can be a good thing.

Getting your baby to sleep

There are different ways for you to get your baby to sleep at night. It depends on your style and the baby's temperament.

There is no easy way to settle a baby to sleep. I will talk about 3 techniques for you to try by reducing contact, by extending the distance between you and by controlled crying, although all involve some degree of crying. It is a personal preference. There are pros and cons to each of the methods.

Reducing contact

Reducing direct contact is the most gentle way to train your baby to sleep on his own. You may have been pacing up and down to settle him so far. Now you want to reduce the physical contact by holding him on a soft mat so that he doesn't get the benefit of physical contact with you, although there is still the motion in place. You can then stop the motion by standing in one place, then go from a standing to a sitting position, then by placing him in the cot if you both can tolerate this. You can pick him up to reassure him if you need to and put him back in the cot as soon as he settles. Repeat as many times as you need to.

It is important that you keep your emotions consistently calm because your baby is sensitive and can pick up any of your stress or frustration, which will make settling him down more difficult. If you are calm by telling him that you love him, telling yourself that you are doing the right thing, you can manage this and do deep breathing exercise, he will eventually find his way to settle. Victory at stage one! You can then continue with the gradual withdrawal (extending distance) technique.

Extending distance

The gradual retreat or camping out technique is another way to train your baby to sleep. You carry out your sleep ritual and leave the room. When your baby cries, you come back and sit or lie down next to his cot (if possible) and stroke him or hold his hand to send him to sleep with minimal words or facial expressions. You then move your chair towards the door by a metre or two but still in the room. Stay there until he falls to sleep. You can then move your chair just outside the door of his room. You can return to your bed in the next room. This method can take more than a week to establish. If he wakes up, you return to the point where he settled to sleep and move away gradually from there onwards. Every couple of nights, you can try to move further away from him. The downside of this practice is that some babies get frustrated and cannot understand why their parent is not picking them up while just sitting there.

Controlled crying

The controlled cry or graduated extinction technique is a controversial practice. Choose the week when you do not have other plans and your older children are on school holiday or staying over at their grandma's. After you perform the sleep ritual, you leave the baby in the cot and leave the room. If he cries, you give it a minute, before you go back in. You try to settle him with as little physical contact as possible. You leave the room again when he settles. If he cries again, you give it 2 minutes, then 5 minutes, then 10 minutes maximum before trying to settle him again. Once the baby realises that whatever he does, you will do the same thing and leave him in his cot, he will get the message and settle, possibly due to exhaustion the first night. You keep doing the same thing again and again so that he will get the message once and for all. Now you have your routine. It normally just takes 3 nights for the baby to get the message.

Some others, in contrast, have suggested that prolonged crying can cause an increase in stress to the baby, hence raising the stress hormone adrenaline and cortisol – an awake hormone that makes settling more difficult. Once the sympathetic nervous system is active, it prepares the body for what is known as the fight-flight response. Accumulated adrenaline can alter the body's function, including elevating blood sugar and quickening the heart rate. The ongoing effect of prolonged crying could cause nervous dysregulation which can be displayed later in life as unhealthy eating or sleep patterns, being anxious, displaying compulsive behaviour, etc. as common symptoms.

If your baby won't fall asleep

When your baby doesn't fall to sleep, you need to identify the problems first following your attempts. Go through the checklist below and add to it if you have found more reasons why he doesn't settle.

Check the obvious reasons first. Is he hungry, thirsty, too cold, too warm, has a dirty nappy, it's too dark, too bright, he is over-stimulated, too tired/in any discomfort? A baby who suffers from reflux or wind, which are the two common conditions in a newborn, may take more time to settle. Has he got a temperature or is he under the weather? Does he just need a cuddle and some reassurance?

For babies with gastric reflux, you can lift the head end of the cot by about 20 degrees. This might help keep your baby's stomach contents down, including the acid. For a windy baby, they probably won't feel comfortable until they burp or pass wind. Try to rotate him periodically by holding him on your forearm and giving a gentle rub or pat on his back.

Was there too much excitement before you settled him, such as a good laugh or giggle with dad when he came home from work? If his body and mind are still excited, he will not be ready for sleep until he has an hour or two quiet time beforehand.

Is there too much excitement around him so that he doesn't really want to miss out? Maybe just tune the noise down a little for him, although it might not be a bad idea for him to get used to some level of noise.

What are the possible solutions? Check what you can do to settle him. Get your own list of things that you know help him. Here is a sample list.

- Feed him more
- Sing a lullaby

- Read a story
- Dim the light
- Leave the corridor light on
- Keep a nightlight in his room
- Pace up and down with him in your arms
- Push him back and forth in his pram
- Take a five-minute drive around town

If he hasn't settled by now, and you feel that your blood pressure is rising, it is safe to leave him in the cot crying for a few minutes and get yourself a cup of tea or have a quick shower to clear your thoughts. You will then have the strength to come back and go through your checklist of soothing methods again. Your baby sometimes senses your stress and anxiety so that you need to calm yourself down first before he feels he's ready to settle.

Now you have got to the end of the checklist and done all the things you could to remedy it, and he may begin to settle. If not, simply start all over again or try to figure out what else could be unsettling him.

It's good to make a note of things that you did to comfort him. Always try what has worked before, although it doesn't always guarantee that it will work the next time.

Chapter 4

Loving Food

"Let food be thy medicine and medicine be thy food."

- *Hippocrates*

We are what we eat so we need to make sure that we are eating well. Good eating habits start from the time of weaning. What would you feed your baby? Do you believe that food can make him ill and food can make him well? Now we know with supporting evidence that poor diet can cause complaints from constipation to more serious conditions like heart disease. Healthy eating habits start at the weaning stage of a baby's life.

You can start to introduce solids to your baby from 6 months of age. However, in special circumstances, such as children with gastric reflux or a severe milk allergy, paediatricians often recommend early weaning from the age of 4 months, as most grandmothers would know.

The World Health Organization promotes breastfeeding to the age of 2 years. Of course, it is your choice when to stop breastfeeding. Most children who I have worked with move on to cow's milk from the age of 1 year.

6 months

Those who have older children might remember that children were given solids from 4 months old a few years ago. You can now move on so much quicker since you start weaning your child from 6 months of age. This is because he is now capable of doing many more things than a 4-month-old child. His organs and digestive system have matured sufficiently to cope with digesting solid foods and its by-product. From the age of 6 months, babies can pretty much digest everything apart from cow's milk as a drink, although you can use cow's milk with cereal or as an ingredient in cooking.

At 6 months, your baby should be able to sit up with minimal support and hold his head up well, and begin to show more interest in food by grabbing your food and putting it into his mouth. He can chew better even with toothless gums and swallow better (just to reassure any anxious mothers), although you should always stay with your baby when he is eating.

Although you should start off giving your child one meal a day, he can soon move on to having 3 meals and 2 snacks such as fresh fruit, rice cakes or vegetable sticks, providing he enjoys it and has good bowel motions.

Find a period of time with little interruption while you are at home to start weaning, so wait until you come back from holiday for example. If you have already started weaning your baby and then go on holiday, you can either take some jars of food that you feel comfortable with or eat good, healthy food provided on holiday, as long as you can tell the chef not to add salt or sugar to the dishes.

Small portions

Start by offering your child small portions such as a couple pieces of fresh banana, a quarter of a piece of buttered toast or some shavings of cheddar cheese on his highchair tray. You can always give him more if he finishes everything. Parents tend to expect their child to take more food than he actually needs. I often hear from parents that their children are not eating well even when they are growing steadily along their percentile chart.

If you are concerned as to whether your child is eating enough, you can pop in to a walk-in clinic and have him weighed. This will give you a clear indication of whether he is eating the right amount. If he continues to gain a satisfactory amount of weight according to his own growth chart (if you are not sure what this is, visit a clinic and your health visitor will explain this to you), and you are giving him a good, balanced diet, you probably do not need to worry.

Feeding too much too fast sometimes can give your child constipation. Allow your child to feed himself as much as possible. By all means, spoon-feed him towards the end of mealtime if he is happy to take a bit more. You should leave him alone if he shows signs of having had enough by turning his mouth away from your spoon, shutting his mouth or throwing food around on the floor.

Allow him plenty of time (up to 60 minutes) to finish his meal. Taking his time to eat will aid his digestion. Remember, mealtime should be fun, so make it enjoyable and let him eat with the family whenever you can. Children want to be part of the crowd. Be aware of your eating behaviour in front of the children because they are very observant. Any grimace or face pulling could make him turn down your offer of food from a spoon.

As your child gets older, you can get him involved in cooking as long as it is safe for his age. I still have very fond memories as a child of making Chinese dumplings. I played with the dough, tried to use a rolling pin and learned to make a parcel with the pastry skin. However, very few survived the boiling water when we were cooking them.

It gave me some idea of how food is prepared before it is put on the table. I remember having a good appetite eating the dumplings that I'd made. You can start by showing your child how to make a sandwich or a bowl of cereal with a splash of berries.

Teach your child about food

If possible, it is a great outing to take your children to visit a farm. Children are naturally curious, so they can make connections and understand their food's journey to the kitchen table, including fish, meat, eggs and poultry. It saddens me when a child tells me that chicken is from Tesco's and pigs live on the television.

Picking fruit or vegetables can be fun for children. You don't have to have access to a farm or orchard or even a garden. It is always possible to grow fruit and veg or herbs in a pot on a windowsill. Involving your children in growing food helps them learn where food comes from and gets them used to eating healthy, fresh food.

Easy-to-grow plants/herbs include cherry tomatoes, peas, strawberries, basil, mint, chives and coriander. Adding some freshly picked thyme to scrambled eggs, basil to a salad, mint to hot water to make a tea, or chives and coriander to a stir fry can transform a meal.

Starting with finger food is the new way of baby-led weaning

Encouraging your baby to feed himself by giving him finger food rather than spoon-feeding him puree is the new way of weaning. This way he can pace himself and stop when he feels full. By doing so, he is given an opportunity to learn to self-regulate, which studies have shown contributes towards a healthy body mass index when he is older.

If he struggles to swallow pieces of finger food, you can chop it up for him or even mash it up with some water. If he is not able to swallow any mashed-up food, then puree can be offered. However, if he struggles with pureed food after some weeks of persevering, you may want to talk to a health visitor about a possible paediatrician referral.

Start as you mean to go on

It is important to establish a healthy eating habit from the beginning. From the start, you can encourage your baby to try a wide range of foods with different textures, flavours and colours – even foods that you might not be so keen on yourself. This makes it more fun for him to experiment with as well as helping him to develop his taste buds and enjoy eating a variety of foods and a well-balanced diet later in life.

Some finger foods ideas that you can try to make a start:

- Avocado slices/fingers.
- Banana discs.
- Sweet potatoes fingers softly boiled or oven baked.
- Apples or pear slices, skinned and cored.
- Soft cooked carrots sticks, green beans.
- Ripe peaches and melon.
- Roasted pumpkin mushed up with some butter.

If your child doesn't like a certain food, you can try again after a couple of weeks. You never know, he might like it next time.

Homemade is best

If possible, it is best to give your baby fresh homemade food so that you know exactly what's in it, i.e. no added salt or sugar, or artificial colours or flavours, and hopefully, everything is fresh with natural flavourings from herbs and spices such as cinnamon, nutmeg, cardamom and vanilla.

Salt

Some parents consider that food has no flavour without salt. You can make a dish tastier by adding herbs and spices. The rest of the family can add table salt to their taste. Although we all need salt in our body, salt is already found in many foods such as bread, cheese, butter, baked beans, etc., so there is no need to add more salt when you are cooking.

Habitually eating salty food as people in many Asian countries do has been positively correlated to high blood pressure, which can lead to many other complications. Hypertension is more common among the Asian population than the white British population, possibly due to this reason. I remember a Filipino father of a one-year-old girl telling me "there is no flavour without salt". He insisted on adding salt to her diet. What he didn't realise is that he was so used to the salty taste, and the whole point is that we want our children to develop a plainer taste so that they grow up to live a healthier lifestyle than us.

Solids and liquids

Once your baby starts eating solid foods, it is best to breastfeed him or give him a bottle after he has eaten. You want him to eat first and drink afterwards so that he doesn't lose his appetite as his stomach fills up with liquid. This could also prevent him from vomiting all the milk up if he gags.

Food will gradually become the main source of his nutrients, while milk will become more like the fluid that you offer him at the dining table. The exact amount children want to drink can vary. As long as he eats well, he should be able to drink as much milk as he wants. If he is no longer interested in milk, you can simply offer yoghurt, cheese or a milkshake made with fresh banana in it to tempt him.

Whole fruit is healthier than juice

When it comes to fruit, it's better to give your baby a piece of whole fruit such as apple, pear or orange to eat, rather than turning the fruit into a puree or juice. The juicing process actually breaks down the cell membranes of the fruit and releases fructose, so that the baby experiences an outburst and surge of sugar rather than the slow release of energy from digesting the fibre in the whole fruit.

If you would like your baby to have some juice, it's best to give it to him at mealtimes, as the saliva produced while eating will reduce the acid from the fruit, which can attack the teeth causing decay.

Protein

Providing the nursing mother is well and healthy, baby will get sufficient amount of protein from breast milk or infant formula. Babies will naturally want less milk to drink once they start eating solids. Instead of only giving children fruit or vegetable purees, it is important to remember to offer them some dietary protein, such as lentils or fish, if you eat these.

Fat

Children under the age of two have different rules from adults in terms of fat consumption. The human breast milk contains 4-6% of fat depending on the mother's diet, which counts towards 20-35% of the baby's calorie intake. This should be continued for the first 2 years. Children need everything full fat as this supplies the nutrients that help with the absorption and metabolism of some nutrients, such as fat-soluble vitamins, which are essential for the growth and development of their organs, such as the brain and nervous system.

Vitamin D

The UK Government recommends that all children should be taking a Vitamin D supplement from the time they are born since there has been an increase in Vitamin D deficiency cases in recent years. In fact, they recommend us all taking it continuously because there isn't sufficient sunshine in the UK, hence, the low production of Vitamin D by the skin. Everyone knows that Vitamin D promotes bone health by helping the body absorb calcium. Vitamin D is also associated with increased autoimmunity and susceptibility to infection.

Fibre

At 6 months, babies get a sufficient amount of fibre from fruit and vegetables plus a couple of spoonfuls of baby rice at each meal to start with. As your baby gets older, you can increase the amount of fibre from starchy food gradually.

Children under the age of two have a slightly different rule from adults in terms of fibre consumption. Unlike adults, who require about 30 grams of dietary fibre in order to have healthy bowels, children require just 15 grams a day.

Wholemeal food can bulk up quickly in their little tummies, making them feel full, so that they end up not getting enough calories or nutrients from other foods. You should avoid wholemeal for children under the age of 2. Wholemeal can also pass through the gut quickly, causing loose stool, which might affect nutrient absorption. You can observe your child's bowel motions and adjust the amount of wholemeal or fruit and vegetables accordingly.

Sugar

Sugar has little nutritional value and it turns our bodies into an acidic environment, where bacteria or fungus can thrive in. Bacteria in the mouth multiply and produce more lactic acid, causing a very acidic pH of 5, which is when tooth decay occurs.

Research has also shown that a more acidic bodily environment is associated with a greater risk of serious health conditions, including type 2 diabetes, heart disease and obesity, while a slightly alkaline environment appears to be linked to improvements in memory and cognition, reduced pain, and the lower risk of high blood pressure and stroke. So keep your child's sugar intake in check.

Model the behaviour you want

Babies and children pick up clues quickly from the people around them – their parents, grandparents, aunts and uncles. So if you want your child to eat a wide variety of healthy foods, you should make sure that you model this behaviour when you eat in front of them.

Be aware of what you say and suggest to your child about food. The foods that he gets used to now will probably become the foods he will eat for the rest of his life.

Case study

I have seen a large number of children with so-called eating difficulties in my 20-year career as a health visitor. However, this little girl left me with the deepest impression.

E was nearly 5 when I went to see her. For the past year, she had eaten barely anything but potatoes. She was under the dietician and paediatrician, and finally was referred to me by her family doctor.

When I met her and her mother at home, her mother eagerly told me in front of the child that "She only eats potatoes". Did you see where the problem was? Yes, the mother had been telling the little girl that "she only eats potatoes", so that's all she would eat. Please revisit the chapter on behaviour to understand exactly how what you say can affect your child.

We played a rainbow game. I said to her "you like rainbow-coloured food, so let's find some food in red colour", and so on. It took a little hesitation before she tucked in and swallowed the first piece of colourful salad, and fed her mother and me at the same time.

I was very pleased and relieved that there was nothing wrong with her. Within 2 hours, she had tried cucumber, tomato and green pepper. Her mother promised to get her some blueberries later.

Taking care of your child's teeth

Most children develop their first tooth at around 6 months, although some are born with teeth and some don't have any until they are almost 2 years old.

When your child first starts teething, you may notice that they dribble all the time and want to chew things, but you probably won't feel the first sharp little tooth for weeks. When they are teething, they love chewing, rubbing and biting onto things, so they can comfortably eat solid food using just their gums.

As soon as you see some teeth coming, commonly the middle bottom two, start brushing them ideally after each meal or in the morning and before bed. Choose toothpaste that contains fluoride for children under the age of 7. They will need your assistance with cleaning until the age of 7 to ensure that their teeth are brushed thoroughly. Once they have a few teeth, you can register them with your dentist at your next visit. Your dentist can advise you if they have any concerns.

Chapter 5

Managing Little Upsets

"Every day, in every way, I'm getting better and better."

- Emile Coue

Parents often talk to me during my home visits or in the clinic about all kinds of minor ailments their children experience. The majority of these require little intervention. Some might simply need over-the-counter medication and home observation.

This chapter describes some of these common ailments and offers suggestions for what you can do yourself to alleviate the symptoms and guidance on when you need to consult your family doctor.

Constipation

Parents often think their new baby is constipated when they observe him pushing with a red face, often crying and kicking his legs.

This behaviour is not necessarily due to constipation. Babies usual strain to go to the toilet or make a big fuss just to pass wind because they have undeveloped abdominal muscles and have yet to grasp how to use them effectively.

Constipation is when the baby's poop appears to be like dry mash potato or, worse, like the shape of a sausage or a pellet, instead of yellow paste, sometimes with pale bits in it.

Most newborns tend to open their bowels frequently once they start feeding properly, usually pooping immediately after each feed due to the short length of their gut and the smaller intestinal surface area. This is particularly true for breastfed babies who tend to do small and frequent poops.

My clinical experience shows that, once they are a few weeks old, some breastfed babies can go up to 5-7 days without opening their bowels, because there is little waste to eliminate according to the textbook. Provided they are content, feeding normally, gaining good weight and having at least 6 wet nappies in 24 hours, there is nothing to be concerned about especially if their poop looks normal once they finally open their bowels.

Breast milk has a natural laxative. It is very rare for breastfed babies to suffer from constipation. In my 20 years' clinical experience as a health visitor, I've only seen 1 or 2 cases of constipation in breastfed babies. If your exclusively breastfed baby is constipated, you need to consult your doctor first to rule out any sensitivity or intolerance or allergy to lactose. In these very rare cases, the mother was advised to stop breastfeeding.

Formula-fed babies tend to open their bowels more regularly. If your formula-fed baby is constipated, first ensure that you are making up the formula strictly according to the instructions because adding too little water or too much powder could lead to constipation. You can also give your baby a mouthful of cool boiled water in between feeds to help move things along.

Rubbing the baby's tummy using a clockwise circular motion or gently moving their legs in cycling motion can often bring relief. If constipation does not ease off or the baby is in distress, then you should consult your doctor.

Diarrhoea

Parents often report that their babies have diarrhoea, based on the number and frequency of bowel movements during a 24-hour period. As I mentioned earlier, breastfed babies can open their bowels after each feed. If the baby is feeding well, doesn't show any signs of discomfort and his poop is like a mustardy paste, he is probably fine and there is no need to be concerned.

If your child's poop is watery, especially if he is more than 1 year or older, you can usually get rehydration medicine over the counter. Providing he is well, comfortable, and eats and drinks normally, you don't need to do anything else. You simply need to ensure that he is hydrated and getting plenty of breast or formula milk, as long as he can keep it down.

If your baby's poop is watery and full of mucus, they don't seem happy, have offensive smelling or strange orangey coloured rather than yellow/light brown poop, or are unable to keep fluids down, it is best to consult your family doctor.

I've learnt over the years that a mother's instinct is more reliable than anyone else's advice, because you know your baby better than anyone else. So follow your instinct.

Vomiting

Another complaint that parents make about young babies is vomiting. A baby's stomach is about the size of a walnut in the first week and grows into the size of an egg by the time they are a month old. Since they are tiny and the muscles that control the contents in and out of the stomach are weak, regurgitation is common among babies. This is also known as posseting. However, if the baby does projectile vomit continuously with poor weight gain, you should consult his doctor urgently.

Gastric reflux

However, if vomiting is associated with discomfort, or is causing weight loss, you should consult your family doctor to rule out gastric reflux. It is generally easy to treat and medication might need to be increased as your baby grows older and gains more weight. Most babies tend to grow out of it by the age of 18 months.

Gastric reflux is an under-diagnosed ailment in my opinion and can cause a tremendous of amount of stress to new parents. A crying baby who won't be soothed by a cuddle from his mother or anyone else may be a sign of gastric reflux or anything else that surely warrants a medical assessment.

The baby might start crying and arching backwards immediately after feeding starts, just as the stomach begins to produce acid to digest the milk. You might also find that the baby has persistent hiccups or coughing.

The reflux baby's vomit often smells acidy (rather than like milk) and this can happen hours after his feed. Gastric reflux can be treated easily by getting prescribed medications from your family doctor.

Apart from putting him on medication, you can help your baby by offering small and regular feeds, regularly burping him during his feed, and by lifting the head-end of his cot up about 15-20 centimetres by putting some books underneath the cot legs.

For formula-fed babies, there are a variety of anti-regurgitant formulas or hypo-allergenic formulas for babies allergic to cow's milk on the market that might help.

Some breastfeeding mothers find it useful to try to alter what they eat. However, the result of such practice can be a restricted diet with a narrow range of foods. Only avoid particular foods if you notice that your baby suffers after you eat them. Otherwise, you should eat a well-balanced diet. If the baby is suffering from gastric reflux, some paediatricians recommend earlier weaning at the age of 4 months, rather than waiting until the usually recommended 6 months.

Parents also need to be aware of silent reflux. This is where you don't see the vomit, but you might notice the baby swallowing when he is lying down or hear a sudden squeal when his stomach contents go up his oesophagus causing burning pain. If your baby appears to cry a lot for no reason and wants to be held all the time, it's worth considering silent reflux and consulting your family doctor.

Ear infections

Reflux babies may have frequent ear infections due to chronic exposure to acidic content. Ear infection is a painful condition. The baby probably would cry a lot and have red cheeks. Occasionally, you might notice that he seems to rub his face with his hand. You can try to manage the condition with an anti-inflammatory such as ibuprofen and see your doctor if there is no improvement or if you notice any discharge from the ear.

High temperature

Providing that your baby looks relatively well and is feeding properly, you can give some paracetamol and ibuprofen alternatively for ailments with a temperature, including teething or ear infection, if trying to cool him down by taking off layers of clothing or blankets and applying a tepid wash prove ineffective.

If there is no improvement after 24 hours, it might indicate a more serious infection if the temperature is persistent, especially if he is feeding less, appears lethargic, is having breathing difficulties, is vomiting or develops a rash. You must consult your doctor immediately. There could be other underlying conditions. Children can deteriorate quickly. If your baby has a persistent high temperature of over 38 degrees Celsius, he needs to be watched over closely.

Rashes

Rashes are very common in young babies because their skin is so delicate and sensitive. Apply baby oil or moisturiser regularly if your baby has dry skin, from daily to a few times a day depending on the severity. It is important to distinguish between blanching rash (which goes pale when you press on it) from a non-blanching rash (which doesn't discolour when you press on it and generally indicates a more serious condition). Regardless of whether the baby looks well or not, a non-blanching rash should be checked by a health professional, so book an appointment with your doctor.

The most often seen rash in newborns are **milia** on the nose, cheeks, forehead, chin or around the eyes – tiny white spots. They are formed from blocked oil glands and disappear on their own in a few weeks because the glands on a baby's face are still developing. If they get infected, then they might need treatment by the doctor, but infections are rare.

Baby acne usually appears on the cheeks, forehead or chin – what causes this is not known. Heat rash shows on the face, chest and back, with small red blanching spots. These are more obviously red when the baby is hot and crying. All you need to do is wash the area with warm water, dab it dry and keep the baby comfortable at the right room temperature (around 19 degrees Celsius), dressing him in a vest and baby grow, and covering him with 2 layers of cotton cellular baby blankets.

Oral thrush

A white coating on the baby's tongue is common; however, if it looks furry and patchy, especially if you notice white patches in the oral cavity or anywhere else, as well as a white-coated tongue, then he probably has oral thrush. You will need to get an antifungal oral treatment from your family doctor.

Oral thrush is a painful condition, which makes the baby want to start and stop feeding, or latch on and off the breast during a feed. It is also commonly related to thrush nappy rash, as it can travel down the gut and affect the other end. If your baby has oral thrush symptoms, you will also need to treat yourself with an antifungal gel applied to your breasts, which you can ask for when you consult your family doctor.

Nappy rash

Nappy rash is another common complaint. The best treatment is to gently clean the area with water, apply a thin layer of barrier cream and expose the skin to the air regularly during the day. If the nappy rash does not improve after 3 days applying the standard treatment described above, or if it worsens, the baby may have thrush nappy rash, which requires an over-the-counter antifungal cream to be applied.

Soft spot

During birth, fontanelles/cranial sutures allow the bony plates of the baby's head to mould over each other for easy passage through the birth canal. The smaller of the two fontanelles, the posterior fontanelle, closes soon after birth, within the first few weeks. The anterior fontanelle or diamond-shaped fontanelle, known as the soft spot on the top of a baby's head, generally takes up to 24 months to close up, meanwhile giving the brain a chance to grow and develop.

The skin covering the fontanelle is quite tough. As a UK-trained health visitor, I advise parents to gently wash the top of the head with water. This might contradict with what some cultures believe. Certainly, in China where I am from, we were advised not to touch the top of a baby's head where the soft spot is, but it is safe to do this.

The soft spot is a good place to monitor whether the baby is dehydrated. If it appears sunken, then he requires more feeds. A bulging soft spot could indicate an increased intracranial pressure that requires immediate medical attention.

Cradle cap

If there is a thick, greasy, crusty layer on top of your baby's fontanelle area, he might have developed cradle cap, which can be quite uncomfortable for him because that is where he loses most heat when he gets hot. You might find him trying to rub or scratch, which sometimes causes small lacerations if the baby has long nails. I always advise parents to soften the crust with white Vaseline, or vegetable or olive oil, overnight or when the baby takes his longest sleep, and then gently brush off any loose crust with an old flannel a few hours later or in the morning. This process might need to be repeated for a few days depending on the thickness of the cradle cap. If the cradle cap looks red, inflamed and smelly, it might indicate infection, in which case, you should consult your family doctor.

Sticky eye

Sticky-eye is another common ailment among young babies. Their eyes can be watery and sometimes crusty. This is commonly caused by a blocked tear duct since these are not fully developed and are very narrow. It can affect one or both eyes.

Providing the conjunctiva (the white part of the eye) is white and the discharge is white or yellow, you can simply clean the eye with a cotton wool ball soaked in cool boiled water, with a single stroke from the inside to the outside corner of the eye. Please also clean the baby's hands to reduce any cross-infection. However, should you notice any redness in the conjunctiva or a green discharge, these are signs of infection and you should consult your family doctor.

Blocked nose

Babies develop blocked noses for various reasons, such as a narrow channel, mucus caused by sensitivity to stimulants in the air, bogeys, etc. No treatment is required generally speaking unless the baby's feeding or sleeping is affected.

If a bogey is blocking the air passage, you can soften it by putting one drop of normal saline from a chemist into the nostril and then gently squeezing the nose to loosen the bogey. Meanwhile, get a small strand of cotton wool and give it a twist. You can use the soft end to tickle baby's nose until he sneezes and then quickly catch what comes out.

Uneven head shape

A baby's head can be moulded unevenly when passing through the birth canal, so sometimes it can look uneven or misshapen after birth. However, here I am talking about an uneven head shape when the baby is around 2-3 months of age.

This often occurs simply from the baby consistently lying in the same position in his cot or other carrier. In particular, if the cot is in his parents' room, the baby will naturally want to watch his parents whenever they are in the same room. This can be corrected either by changing the position of the cot which is not always practical in a smaller bedroom or by changing the baby's head and feet position in his cot so that he has to turn his head in the opposite direction to look at his parents.

If you think that the baby is unable to move his head from one side to the other, he might require some physiotherapy. Your family doctor can refer you to a suitable physiotherapist. Some parents have purchased a special helmet to correct the baby's head shape. Baby has to wear it 23 hours a day, which I believe to be cruel. Misshaped head would become rounder as he gets older and sits up more. Once he grows more hair, it would be unnoticeable.

Chapter 6

Love and Acceptance

"You can't teach children to behave better by making them feel worse. When children feel better, they behave better."

- Pam Leo

I didn't sign up for this – how to manage challenging behaviour

This chapter explains why children behave the way they behave, how to manage challenging behaviour by using the correct response and language, and how to encourage your child to behave the way you want them to behave. The better you understand him, the easier you will find how to guide him to the behaviour you want him to display.

Understanding children's brainwaves at different developmental stages

Birth to 2 years

Each child develops at their own pace. However, generally speaking, between birth and 2 years of age, children's brains function primarily in the lowest brain-wave cycle, that is 0.5 to 4 cycles per second. These are called Delta waves as seen on an EEG (electroencephalogram) – which are the same waves experienced when we as adults are in deep sleep.

Children at this age are typically sleepwalking even when they are awake. They are like "a bull in the China shop", crashing into things or diving into danger without the awareness of themselves or their environment. They do not yet have the brain faculty to analyse, judge or think.

Although children have their own genetic makeup, they are also very much influenced by the nurturing of their parents or anyone who they spend a significant amount of time with. Before the age of 2, children are receptive to changes and new things in their lives. They are yet to have developed the concept of me, others or gender. They have no fear or sense of danger and little understanding about rules, so they feel free to take part and get involved in activities or groups. It is helpful at this age to spend regular time at a playgroup or pre-school nursery, meeting some new people rather than just seeing family members.

Children at this age love to be the centre of the show and know exactly how to get your attention. They do not distinguish whether you are shouting at them or cheering for them. They want attention of any kind and they are satisfied with themselves when they cause a reaction. For them, it is like repeatedly pressing the button on a toy to make the moo cow pop out and make a noise. So when you react to their behaviour, they want to keep pressing the same button to see the reaction again, because they are fascinated by the moment that they have made something happen.

When your child of up to 2 years feels that he is being ignored, particularly at a time when you are busy with something or someone, he can get upset that he is being left out. Frustration can also be experienced for his not being understood or being able to understand you, especially before the development of sufficient speech and language skills. You have to be patient and train your child by loving him, accepting him, directing him, guiding him, supervising him and catching him when he falls.

Challenging behaviour can be normal and healthy

It's normal for children to show challenging behaviour as they're growing and developing, and pushing boundaries with their newly found mental and physical abilities.

It's important to see things from your child's perspective. Understanding what he is like and what he knows. He obviously doesn't have the same level of intelligence, knowledge and life experience as you've gained over the past 20, 30 or more years. Hence, he doesn't get your point of view. You need to have the right level of expectation that is appropriate for the age of your child.

2 to 5 years

From about 2 to 5 years of age, children begin to demonstrate slightly higher EEG brain wave patterns, which can be measured between 4 to 8 cycles per second. These brain waves are called Theta waves. Theta waves are the twilight state in which adults can find themselves half awake and half asleep. Children at this age live in the realm of imagination, daydreaming and showing no signs of critical, rational thinking.

This is a very impressionable state. Everything anyone says to your child goes into his little head. This is also a super learning state where children are like a sponge that absorbs fully of all the information presented to them subconsciously. They are open to suggestions. They are likely to accept what you tell them as true. People in a Theta brain wave state seem like they are under a hypnotic trance in which their inner world seems more real than their outer world.

Between the age of 2 to 3, children grow and develop so fast, and meet a number of milestones. They become physically strong, able to run, climb, kick and throw. They feel more confident in their abilities. They sometimes even feel that they can conquer the world. For those who have older children, do you remember the time when your child was pushing your hands away when you tried to hold him or protect him? He wanted to be independent and do everything himself, his way.

Two to 3 year olds also become mentally strong by developing their own little characters and developing a sense of self while taking on your values, beliefs, rules and standards, and your judgement. This is the period where you are programming his mind. Yes, just like a technician programs your computer, so be aware of what you want to put into your child's head, because he could end up running this programme automatically for many years to come.

Children become more aware of self and others after 2 years. If your child now stands in front of the mirror, he is aware that the one in the mirror is himself. He can tell you all his body parts and become aware of the differences between the sexes. Your child now knows that he is a boy or a girl. Since their personalities have become more apparent and they speak more fluently, children at this age now behave more like a mini adult.

Wouldn't it be nice if your child always behaved the way you wanted them to behave?

Yes and no.

Yes. It would avoid a great deal of struggle and stress, and save you a lot of headache and possibly heartache, if your child always behaved the way you wanted them to behave.

But no, you don't want that. A child who only does what they're told lacks initiative and enthusiasm, and is likely to grow into an adult who has no passion for life and who drifts in whichever direction the wind is blowing.

So how can you get your point across to him?

Positive instructions work better than negative instructions. First of all, you need to keep your instructions simple, clear and positive. As explained above, children are not responsive to negative instructions. They don't hear the words 'no' or 'don't' very well. They just hear the action word and act it out. So choose your action words carefully.

One day I was travelling by train to London. It was the summer holidays, so there were lots of families with young children on the train. In particular, there were three people sat opposite me – a little boy about four years old, his mother and his grandmother. The little boy started poking his mother's nose while the two women were chatting away and totally ignoring him. He got his mother's attention straightaway. "Don't poke my nose," she said. He poked it again. "Don't poke my nose, I said," she repeated, raising her voice in frustration. But he kept on poking.

It was natural for the mother to react this way. Her child's behaviour was very annoying and interrupting her conversation. But from the child's perspective, he was just having fun and getting his mother's attention, which he was missing.

She could have done one or two things to stop him poking her. She could have recognised that he needed a bit of attention. Or she could have given him a positively phrased instruction explaining what she wanted him to do – for example, "I'm talking to grandma right now. How about sitting down and reading your book until we're finished."

It's important to give your child an instruction that he can carry through. Often, parents say what they don't want, and don't state clearly what they do want. Telling a child to 'behave' can be confusing for him. He doesn't always know what you mean by 'behave'. So if you're dealing with challenging behaviour, take a moment to pause and think about what you'd like your child to do now instead of what he is doing that you don't approve of. Then tell him clearly and simply. Be aware exactly what you say and how you say it to your child.

If this is some behaviour that you do not want to see in the future, you mustn't react. You need to keep the same gesture, posture and your mouth shut as if you did not see it. If you have the urge to tell him off, you want to say a quick "no" or shake your head with an indifferent face, then quickly bring his attention to something that you do want him to do. At this time, you need to give good eye contact with a warm relaxed or an animated facial expression and a soft, higher-pitched tone of voice.

As parents, it's so automatic for us to add "no" in front of what we don't want to see, such as, "don't run" or "don't spill the water". Children don't process "no" well; instead, they are more likely to pick up the words after "no".

Some parents even have mistaken saying "no" as good parenting and use a great deal of it. In the end, "no" has no meaning attached to it. Plus every time you say "no" to something, you have just brought your child's attention to the very thing that you do not want him to do. If you say it often, all he remembers is the very thing that you do not want him to do. It becomes meaningless. I have also seen children give their parents a smile and carry out exactly what they don't want them to do. You really want to keep "no" to a minimal. Instead, tell them what you do want them to do.

It's kind of straightforward when you want them to do something. But when you want them to stop doing something, you must think of something else for them to do. It's more difficult for children to do nothing and easier just to ask them to do something else, even if the command is to read a book. With a bit of practice, speaking positively will come naturally.

Below are a few examples of positive instructions:

Instead of saying:	Say:
Don't throw a ball in the room	Let's roll the ball on the floor or Let's take the ball outside.
Don't drop the cup	Hold the cup with both hands.
Don't run	Walk slowly and carefully.
Don't shout	Let's talk quietly or Can you speak quietly (remember to demonstrate). Let's whisper.
Don't hit her	We give our friends cuddles and kisses.
Don't spill the water	Hold the cup steadily.
Don't be rude	You are polite and say please and thank you.
Don't leave a mess	You tidy up everything once you finish your play.
Don't be late for school	You want to get up early enough to have time for breakfast and go to school on time like your school friends.

People understand positive statements better than negative or double negative statements. Children in particular, with their developing brains, find it much easier to digest the message if you make a positive statement and tell them nicely and directly what you want them to do.

It is alright if you realise that you said the wrong thing. Interrupt yourself, press an imaginary reset button, change your words or behaviour, and get back on track again. The more you practise, the easier it gets.

Model the behaviour you want in your children

For most of us, and for children especially, our visual modality is more dominant, so that we learn by observing and acting out what we see more than what we hear. Therefore, it's not surprising that children tend to do what you do and not necessarily what you tell them to do.

Children are very observant between 2-5 years. They learn fast how to achieve what they want.

One day during one of my home visits, a mother told me a story about her daughter J who was 4. She said that J cried a lot more since the arrival of her new baby sister. When the mum asked J why she was crying, something that she had stopped doing since she could talk when she was 2, J replied: "You always go to the baby and pick her up straightaway when she cries. I want you to come to me and give me a hug when I cry." J got what she wanted – her mum back.

The above example has just proven a simple point that a child will observe accurately what works, what doesn't and knows exactly what he needs to do to get what he wants.

A star-chart works miracles at this pre-school stage. You can use all the free papers and flyers that come through your door, cut them into stars or shapes to stick on a homemade chart. As a reward for achieving a certain number of stars, you can use the purchase of essentials such as a pair of socks, pants as incentives or rent a video, a book, or go on a picnic so that your child feels so proud that he has earned it for being helpful.

Master your emotions

Some basic tips on how to change your emotional state are discussed earlier in Chapter two: Love and Connection and in Chapter ten: Self-Parenting.

You know when you are in a better emotional state, you are more tolerant and say what you mean; but when you are under stress, you might overreact and come up with anything at the spur of the moment that you might regret later. Have you heard these examples? "You can never eat another sweet again" (if he has finished the whole jar). "I shall leave you on the train if you are not moving fast" (if he is slow to get off). "If you only eat potatoes, you might become one, one day."

The behaviour is usually triggered by a thought that triggers an emotion that triggers a chain of neurological responses and chemical changes in your body to produce what you have just said. Using the example from above, if you are watching your child eating lots of sweets or carbohydrates, this may trigger a fear in you of him becoming say overweight like yourself.

His behaviour has touched a sensitive spot in your nervous system, a memory that is linked to a sorrow and angry story from that part of your life, so you have overreacted. At that moment, you are not living in the present. You are thinking of your past and his future, and what is true for you might or might not be true for him.

You are so worried about your child so that you shouted out the very thing that you do not want him to become because you were running on autopilot. When you are in fear, you become narrowly focused. You can only think of one thing – in this case, carbs to obesity, rather than taking into account the level of exercise he is doing and his age and the demands of his body.

So thoughts, feelings and behaviour are totally connected. You can simply stop the loop by being aware of what you are thinking, feeling and doing. If you don't like what you have just said, you can stop yourself in your tracks by changing direction once you have noticed that you are having negative thoughts that are leading you down the same old path. Pause for

5 seconds, think about what you do want and express that thought accordingly, such as "mum really wants you to be healthy and strong. You should have more fruit and vegetables." Apologise to your children if you have made a mistake.

It might sound counterintuitive, but the key is to learn to manage your own emotional state and your behaviour. Children sense your emotions, which project out like signals that trigger their subconscious programme to simply mimic you.

You need to set a good example for your child. Influence and lead your child by example, because he will model you. Shouting at your child to be quiet sends a conflicting message. If you want your child to speak quietly, you should lower your voice, and slowly and clearly say "Let's speak quietly". This way, he will understand what you mean by "quiet" and will naturally mimic your behaviour.

I remember talking to a mother about her son's behaviour problem. When I arrived at the house, she shouted from the bottom of the stairs: "Come down, the health visitor is here. When he came down, she said aggressively: "Sit there and listen." I later asked her whether she would talk to her husband like this. She said, "Of course not". I explained the way she talked to her child sounded very much like a command like you would talk to a dog, but without warmth. So the child was really just modelling the way that his mother behaved. He was mirroring her.

If there is any behaviour you don't like to see in your child, you must look at yourself first. Rather than looking at how to change him, look at what you could do to change yourself. Once you have changed how you behave, your child is going to change guaranteed. You might not get it right the first time round and that is perfectly alright. It can be a process of trial and error or tweaking your actions until you achieve what you want to achieve.

Where to set the boundaries

It is healthy to have boundaries so that your child knows what is expected of him, but do remember to loosen those boundaries as he grows and develops.

Children need boundaries. With boundaries, they feel comfortable and secure. But where should you set the boundaries very much depends on your child, because all children are different, as well as your tolerance threshold. The bottom line is that you both must feel happy with the boundaries set.

In order for your child to achieve his best, the boundaries should be set just slightly outside his comfort zone. Like wearing a pair of new shoes, you want to give some room for development. It's like when he was learning how to walk, he fell so many times, but you made sure you were there to catch him.

Although there aren't any prescribed boundaries per say, there are some general guidelines. If one of you is not happy about a boundary, then you need to explore other possibilities, explain what you want simply and lovingly, so that your child gets your point, while you listen to his. As your child grows and develops, the boundaries can be relaxed and adjusted appropriately in line with his mental and physical development.

Be consistent

Just as you thought you had cracked it, suddenly, it seems to all come crashing down or going backwards. This is part of the process. Be patient. Recognise that there will be steps forward and steps backward. Don't dwell on any setbacks; instead, move on and move forward with consistency.

It's important to have a consistent parenting style so that your child is clear about what is expected of him. So make sure that you and your partner both present a united front. Disagreeing in front of your child is very confusing and distressing for him. He may want to take sides with one parent but feel bad and disloyal towards the other. This could result in a behaviour problem – a child's strategy for saving his parent's relationship. If you two disagree about how to parent, you must resolve your disagreements when your child is not around – ideally before he is born.

We were all brought up differently by our own parents – perhaps even with different values, rules and beliefs. So it's not uncommon for parents to have different parenting styles. For example, one parent may think that it's okay for the child to ride his bicycle on the street to "learn road safety", while the other parent may think it's too dangerous.

There isn't a right way or a wrong way. It very much depends on your child's ability and character. You know your child better than anyone else. So what does he like doing? What is he good at? How can you encourage his creativity and bring the best out of him?

Supportive environment

It's also important that the other people and environments that your child experiences don't conflict with the environment you create at home. Try to find childminders, day-care, nurseries, etc. that do things in a similar way to you and reflect your priorities.

What to do if your child hits another child

If your child hits another child, you can say a firm "no" while lowering your voice and looking sternly into his eyes so that it is clear to him that his behaviour is unacceptable. Then describe and demonstrate the behaviour you expect of him, for example, by saying "We give our friends cuddles and kisses". You can then offer cuddles to him and to his friends. If he copies you and cuddles his friends, you can reinforce the good behaviour by making a big fuss of him and giving him positive feedback.

To summarise, here are the 5 simple principles for creating the desired behaviour in your children

- Say what you mean and want. Lead by example
- Be present for them to model you
- Be responsive when they need you
- Be tolerant when they make mistakes
- Be forgiving with love from your heart

Practise the simple principles, keep practising

The principle of behaviour management is so simple. But are you practising what you know? Are you being consistent? It takes tenacious awareness and continuous action to keep making progress towards where you want to be.

Chapter 7

Learning Through Play

"*Do not train a child to learn by force or harshness; but direct them to it by what amuses their minds, so that you may be better able to discover with accuracy the peculiar bent of the genius of each.*"

*- **Plato***

There has been a tremendous amount of research by psychologists into the value of teaching and learning through play or play-based learning.

I cannot emphasise enough of the importance of play in a child's life, as a health visitor. To a child, everything is new and everything can be playful, including the mischievous. Play is fun time. It is the time when you can bond with your child, building trust and developing friendship. Play is how children experience the world, through what they know and what they are about to find out, by finding out what they are capable of and learning what they dare to venture.

Being Chinese, my upbringing was very restricted – it was all about study and hard work. I feel that I missed all the fun and missed all the lightness in life. I had to learn how to have fun and how to play after I started working in the field with children. My nursery nurse colleagues were excellent in bringing in their creative ideas and showing me that everything can be a toy, as long as that you provide appropriate supervision, including for a baby to touch a bicycle metal chain lock or putting spaghetti through his fingers. I am forever grateful for their genius in creativity, which has opened up my mind to a world of fun that encourages me to continuously explore and learn about the world around. You are never too old to play and there is always time for fun. Life should be fun.

"Time you enjoy wasting is not wasted time."
- T.S. Elliot

Learning is made easy when a child is relaxed, shows interest and curiosity in a subject, and when he is totally absorbed in the present moment in whatever he is doing. By discovering the world around him, he begins to formulate his own opinions and views of the world. In the early years, he grows and develops, and his physical and mental ability is soaring. Something he couldn't do yesterday, he now can do. He is proud of himself with that victorious smile on his face. Remember that moment when he was able to stand up on his own feet and take the first step? Remember that look on his face?

Being a child, he only knows about the end result, the winning. He does not care about the 100 times he fell down, but celebrates with the joy, a big smile on his face when he is finally able to stand up and walk. Most adults have forgotten the inner child inside of us crying out for fun and joy. We seem to have taken life too seriously and can't remember that after all the falls, there is winning in the end if you just keep going, learning and improving your skills. So keep going after what you love and don't settle for anything less.

Play needs to be developmental age appropriate.

In this chapter, I have grouped a child's physical mental development into different stages, what's appropriate for him to play with to bring the most benefit and how you can ensure his safety around those activities. It's almost impossible to separate the above issues. Everything is connected, so it's not easy to talk about one thing without mentioning the other. As he develops, what used to excite him will now no longer attract his attention. Then it's time to up the game.

The first 3 months

Foetus can hear perfectly well through the amniotic fluid in your womb, as research suggests. He could even feel your emotions in the uterus, although he is not yet to be able to express them or communicate them to you clearly. 4D ultrasound footage showed a foetus had startling movement when the mother shouted, although she would not necessarily felt it that if it wasn't for the monitoring on at that time.

Newborns appear to be doing very little else apart from feeding and sleeping. In fact, they can hear perfectly well. Your newborn baby apparently would calm down if you play music or listen to your favourite radio station – the one that you listened to during your pregnancy.

He sees short distances of less than a foot at birth, extending to about a metre as he grows, and loves bright colours such as yellow and red, natural or artificial lights, and various shapes with strong contrasts, such as black and white hanging objects.

Do move things around or change his position in the cot to ensure that he develops a rounder-shaped head as well as balanced eye muscle development.

From 1 month onwards, he will become more alert. He will begin to show some responses and reactions to being picked up or talked to. He will enjoy a bit more time being upright so that he has a better perspective on his world, while you support the back of his neck and head.

How he experiences the world during this period is predominantly through hearing, touching, tasting and smelling. He will turn toward sounds or be startled when it's too loud. Soft music, radio, storytelling or simply chatting to him, having a cuddle or being stroked are all play for him at this stage. So make it fun. He learns about you and all the significant others by absorbing everything around him, such as how he is handled, fed, changed and soothed. For instance, when he wants a feed and he hears your soft voice and smells your milk that reassures him.

For now, as long as he is gaining weight, on average 1 kilogram each month (up to 4 months), he is doing alright. Baby safety we have already discussed extensively earlier in Chapter 1 Coming Home, so that I won't repeat it here.

3-6 months

He enjoys his bedtime routine listening to a story or nursery rhymes told in a soft and warm tone of voice before he falls to sleep. He can see a lot better. He is able to follow a dangling object or follow you around a room with his vision. He begins to copy your facial expressions and gestures, for instance, if you poke out your tongue, he will do the same. He begins to mirror you by smiling and cooing back if you smile and talk to him habitually. Talking to your baby using vivid facial expressions, holding good eye contact and making faces is a great game for him to watch.

Babies who receive less stimulation may experience a delay in social smiling, which is a developmental milestone. Children with a visual impairment may not smile because they are not able to see or mimic you. The family doctor should pick this up if there is any abnormality of the eyes/vision, at his regular developmental reviews.

He will get excited, smile or stop crying when he sees that you are getting ready for his feed. He learns all the cues for feeding, such as how you hold him and putting a muslin sheet under his chin. He often smiles at your face when he anticipates something pleasurable like a feed or a bath. Having a bath with his older siblings becomes fun. He can utter some vowel sounds such as "a" or "o", cooing sounds and gurgle when you are conversing with him in baby talk – a high-pitched made-up voice.

He has now developed more voluntary control of his arm movements and actively interacts with what's around him. He has developed a degree of hand and eye coordination so he reaches out to grasp toys he can see in his baby gym, catches a glimpse of himself in the dangling mirror, shakes a rattle and kicks a toy that makes a funny noise and excites him. He feels the different textures, listens to the crackling noises when he squeezes a gym toy or accidently records and plays back his own voice by pressing the heart of a teddy bear. He expresses his pleasure when being picked up with playful kicks and arm movements.

Once he sees something attractive by his side, he will attempt to roll over and make an effort to move towards it. This is a good exercise for him to practise. Your baby is now on the move voluntarily, so make sure that he is in a cot or a playpen when unsupervised. He might begin to roll onto his front around 4 months of age. If he is not rolling by 6 months, you need to talk to your health visitor, who can provide you with some exercises to do at home, before you need to worry about any physical problems. In many cases that I have seen, children who lay on their backs all the time might have some delay in their motor skills at this stage.

Once he is able to roll onto his front, you can leave him on his front to sleep because it's impossible for you to keep putting him back on his back all night long. Since he has developed the ability to roll, he is now also able to do so many other things, such as pushing his upper body up or getting your attention by making a loud noise.

6-12 months

At a glance, he can sit unassisted, crawl or bottom shuffle, pull to himself to standing, take his first step or walk along furniture, utter his first consonant sounds before a vowel sound, making his first word for example "ma" or "da". This makes parents so happy and proud. He can wave "bye-bye", understands his name, finger points to what he wants, has a pincer grasp and can feed himself. He begins to feel shy with strangers and gets excited when familiar adults appear. Most children at this age still have a nap during the day and are able to sleep through the night, which only means that physically he no longer requires a feed at night.

I have seen babies that never crawled but moved from sitting to standing and walking. When I say crawl, I mean that it could be all kinds of combinations, such as one-armed commando-style or wriggling backwards.

Unlike most parents have envisaged, a baby would crawl on all fours and move forward.

He is on the move. The best play to encourage gross motor development is to give him space on the floor or outside on the lawn for him to move around freely, roll, crawl, sit and pull himself to standing. He learns to cruise along a sofa or take his first step towards one year of age. He loves to explore and get his hands on things, so move things up or out of reach if there is anything that you don't want him to touch.

He might still have difficulties in sitting back down initially. With practice, he will gradually learn to let go of the hands and collapse to his knees to get back down on his bottom to a sitting position.

He now almost sees the world as well as you do. Combined with his newly found pincer grasp ability using his finger and thumb, he is now able to pick up all the crumbles on your floor. He also learns by putting everything into his mouth from 6 months onwards, so your days of second-to-second supervision have to start now, I always tell parents, because accidents happen in a split second.

You baby has now also started eating solid foods. He has no idea what's edible and what's not. He is trying out things by putting them in his mouth – everything. I have had numerous A+E reports of children who have eaten slugs in their garden or cat biscuits from the pet bowl.

He is like a health and safety inspector and can discover the most hidden dust or fluff on the carpet, find the coin behind the sofa and a dropped tablet by your bedside table. Any of the new things that he has found could end up in his mouth. So make sure you carry out your inspections before he does. Get down on your knees so that you see what he sees.

He has a fascination about gaps and holes and likes to put his finger in them. He loves shaking and banging deliberately to make a sound. Objects that are breakable, such as a glass table, glass doors or a television screen, should be laminated. Get a safety pack from your home store to cover them up or move them out of his reach.

He can now grasp his bottle or cup with his hands and is able to reach to grab food off your plate and put it into his mouth. He has also learned how to open his palm and let things go. Where do things go once they leave my palm? That fascinates him. He follows a dropping object onto the floor. You pick it up and he drops it again. It's only a game. This can be food that he is dropping when he is feeling full.

If you travel by car, you now need to keep an eye on the weight limit and height restrictions by the car seat manufacturer. It is the safest position for him to sit rear facing. You should only change him to forward facing when you have to.

He loves books, is able to turn thick pages, presses a button that plays a tune, and cuddles a soft toy to give him soothing and comforting effect. Your household cooking utensils such as a saucepan, a wooden spoon, sweet wrappers or even a heavy metal bike lock chain can be played with under close supervision. Old mobile phones, ends of the toilet roll or even an old water bottle with some dry pasta twists inside or filled with water with washing up liquid and glittering star floaters can be used as toys.

Children like to have a variety of things to play with in order to keep them interested. Share toys with your friends, hire toys from a local toy library and get toys from a charity shop or anything in your household that you consider safe for him to play with under supervision. Be creative.

This is an exciting time for him to learn so many new things. He openly demonstrates delighted responses to active playful chat and exciting movements. He particularly enjoys a peek-a-boo game at this stage because what he can't see, he thinks has disappeared. He is so excited when you remove the veil and he is reunited with his familiar surroundings and usually has a good giggle.

Most delays in a child's development are identified in the first year, for example, if the child has problems rolling, sitting unsupported, bearing weight in his knees and standing up with support; if he can't feed himself with finger food; if he doesn't start to make "ma" and "da" sounds, smile and respond to his name, or if you have any other concerns about any aspects in his development.

Health visitors routinely carry out reviews of children's growth and development at 1 year. If you have missed any of these appointments or have concerns, simply get in touch by taking your child to a local clinic or consult your doctor for a referral.

1-2 years old

Your child continues to develop his large muscle skills by crawling, toddling, climbing onto a sofa or up the stairs. Children are creative. One little girl pulled the drawers out in the kitchen unit and used them to climb up to the kitchen top, which surprised her mother. Rather than saying "he is not doing that yet", think a step ahead of his ability because he will always surprise you with what he is capable of.

Should you need to leave your child unsupervised for instance to go to the bathroom or answer the door, you should leave him in a child-proof area in your home or younger children under the age of 2 can be left in a travel cot or a playpen just for a brief duration when you have to do something without them. When he is older than 2, when he may attempt to climb or unlock the safety gate; you simply need to take him with you. He now recognises familiar adults and may not be happy to be left with strangers.

The best play to encourage fine motor development is to let him feed himself with his fingers, a spoon or a fork, or hold a pen to scribble or colour. Allowing him to pick up small crumbs off his feeding table will help him with his pincer grasp, transferring food between his hands, and developing hand and eye coordination by putting food into his mouth.

Your child can further improve his fine motor skills by playing with Lego, shape-sorters or other building blocks, clapping his hands when singing, playing a keyboard or plucking an instrument, holding a crayon with a palmer grasp to scribble or colour, and zipping and unzipping his coat.

In my clinical experience, I have not seen any children with isolated fine motor skill delays. In general, fine motor delays tend to be part of the global delay. So you probably would have noticed abnormalities in other areas first such as his ability to roll or sit.

Before the age of 2, children are more receptive to changes and new things in their lives. They are yet to have developed the concept of me, others or gender. They have no fear or sense of danger and little understanding of rules, so they feel freer to take part and get involved. It is the perfect time to participate more in local parents groups or at the gym crèche so that he learns to interact with others, adults or children.

Child-led play

Experience helps him develop imagination. He is now able to self-select toys that he wants to play with. He can make his wishes known by finger pointing when he wants something. The more places he has been, the more activities he has done, the clearer he will be about what he wants to play with when it comes to child-led play time, such as dress-up time, so anything in your wardrobe that you are happy to let go of can be put in the dress-up box.

With his ever faster increasing motor skills, cognitive skills and leadership skills, this allows him to freely express himself and use his imagination to the full. It can also reveal what he loves doing and is good at. He will feel most satisfied when he has 30 minutes in a day when he can tell you what he wants to do or show you what he wants to play with. You don't need to say anything apart from acknowledging and agreeing to his wishes (unless it's dangerous). Allow your child to tell you what he wants to do and what he wants to spend time on.

Child-led play is the most beneficial form of play which develops a child's true character. The parent's role is to uncover his talent. You can start child-led play as early as you notice that he is taking the lead. This type of play allows him to deeply and fully immersed in his own world, to utilise his imagination even if it doesn't make sense to you. You simply follow his command during playtime. Let him lead. He might do what you have done or act out what he has seen or heard, such as making you a cup of tea or giving his teddy bear a cuddle.

During child-led play, he can play with what he wants and learn naturally, explore with his 5 senses, and grow and develop at his own pace. You decide the length of the playtime. It's better to use a simple command to signify the start and the end so that he learns that this is his time such as "playtime" and "finished". So that he gradually learns when you say "playtime", he can tell you what to do. When you say "finished", everything reverts back to how it is normally, so what you say goes and he follows. Over time, if you are consistent, he will get a clear message and things will become easier.

Before language develops, he may experience frustration because he is not understood and his needs are not met or he doesn't understand what is expected of him. You can use gestures; some parents have combined baby signing and verbal communication at this stage of their child's learning. However, there isn't clear evidence that children develop overall better language skills later by learning baby signing first.

2-3 years

Remember everything is play, everything is learning for him as he is fast developing his mental and physical abilities. "Danger", for a toddler, is a "game" as everywhere in the home environment are things that he is not allowed to touch or play with. He will try to climb to reach objects without the ability to assess the stability of what he steps onto. He will stand on a convenient "item" on the sofa to look out of the window, without knowing that it is his baby sister who is too fragile to carry his weight. He will share his food with his newborn sibling because mum has taught him to share.

Overall, most parents tend to have prepared well for their children's safety in the home. Most accidents actually happen when you visit others and you don't know what they have in their home environment, such as a pond or a pet. Be extra vigilant when you are out and about.

At this age, your child will begin to do simple puzzles, learn nouns and his body parts, read picture books, colour a book, sing songs, dance to a tune, mimic a policeman with his hat on, help you to bake a cake or make a sandwich or play a simple musical instrument. Sitting on the potty and reading books is play for him. Some musical potties even play a tune when a child pees.

He will love to help you load the washing machine, put the shopping away or plant flower borders. He is so keen and helpful at this stage and will do most things with you. The list is endless. Be creative as long as it is under your supervision and guidance, bearing in mind at all times that it is safe for his age and development.

He is full of energy and enjoys the outdoors and explores the world around him. He gets bored quickly and likes to move around to the next thing. Physical activities such as walking, running, climbing, swimming, cycling, dancing to music, skipping or kicking, throwing or catching a ball help to develop the large groups of muscles in the body, specifically, in the legs, buttocks, shoulders and arms. Some children, especially those who were born prematurely or who were ill as newborns, might be overprotected by their parents during the early years and do little physical exercise.

Before starting school is a good time to help your child pick up physicals skills, if conditions allow, as it will help to improve his cardiovascular health, bone health, strengthen muscles, and develop movement and coordination. Participating in these activities will also help him join in and feel part of the group during exercise time when he is at school. Get him interested in new things by providing opportunities. It's like opening doors for him so that he knows that these things exist, although by no means make him go through these doors if he is not ready.

When children speak

Around the age of 2 years, children begin to understand the meaning of words and develop a bank of vocabulary of 20 words. By 3 years, they should know about 50 words. Most children can string 2 to 3 words together such as "daddy car" or "mummy work" or "see you later", but also talk a lot of gibberish sentences. They will defend anything in their hands even if it is not theirs. Everything becomes "Mine".

The most important thing to remember is whether they understand you and can follow simple commands like "get your coat" or "put your shoes on". Familiar adults tend to be able to understand them first, a lot earlier than new people, including grandparents who don't see them often or nursery teachers who have just met them.

If neither you nor your partner speaks English, you should speak to your child in your native language. Your child will pick up English quickly when he starts nursery or school. I often see children who have grown up in multi-lingual families. They tend to answer back in English especially those with older siblings or once they start nursery/school, regardless what language you use to ask them questions in the first place.

When you should be concerned

There are a number of situations where you may want to consult a health visitor. These include:

- Your child plays alone focused on a single activity happily for hours without disrupting you. You might think this is great as you can have all the time you need to do what you think is important, but it is unusual behaviour for a toddler.
- He is very active, moving around spending no time sitting down doing activities like scribbling, colouring or building with Lego or doing puzzles, especially if he has poor eye contact, poor speech and language skills with very few single words and he doesn't have a good understanding of simple commands.
- He appears to make involuntary noises or

movements of the limbs when he gets excited.

- He is a fussy eater and will only have a particular coloured or shaped food.
- There is no finger pointing and he grabs your hand when he wants something.

The health visitor will carry out an initial assessment of your child's development, give you advice to help him with his speech and language development or refer him to an audiologist for a hearing test, a speech therapist and/or a community paediatrician, if necessary.

3-5 years

Your child can now stand on one leg, jump forward with both feet together, skip, climb the stairs like an adult, knows the colours and counts numbers, and can build a tower with ten Lego bricks using his dominant hand, build a bridge with three bricks and put a crayon underneath pretending to be a passing boat. He can sit astride a bicycle, cycling off with his helmet on.

It is important to introduce colours after he has learnt about the basic nouns. Otherwise, he might call every car he sees a "red car". Likewise, you should teach your child manners after he grasps the basic nouns. If you insist on him saying "Thank you" when you offer him an apple, he might think "Apple" is actually called "Thank you".

Children by this age have developed a vast amount of physical, motor and cognitive skills. They begin to understand the concept of time. They are more sociable, more independent and self-willed. They sometimes behave like a mini adult and desire to be treated like one with respect. Although their behaviours are more sensible, they can now argue with words and demand an explanation or justification. They are keen to take care of younger siblings and more aware of dangers; however, they still require one hundred percent of your supervision.

You can begin to introduce sports such as tennis, skiing, golfing, and boating. We all know sports personalities who began their careers this early and started to show talent and their unique genius.

Your child lives in a world of imagination at this stage and would introduce you to his imaginative friends and make up stories. He enjoys dramas and role-plays by ordering you about like a pupil while he acts like a teacher during child-led-play. He is able to hold a pen like a tripod, drawing circles, triangles or crosses with more complex lines. He learns paper folding and cutting with scissors to happily make his own star chart that encourages good behaviour. You can also introduce him to your hobbies like bird watching, star gazing, fishing, caring for a pet, collecting insects or bugs, growing herbs, baking or gardening.

Why not try staying on a farm, picking eggs and milking a cow, or fruit picking? Children now also enjoy more social events such as birthday parties. Try out different modes of transportation, learn about cultures and taste different food, and do people watching together.

When children are around the age of 2, they tend to play alongside each other, with the occasional fight for the same toy. However, as children get older, usually after the age of 3, they begin to communicate more with one another, become more aware of the others around them, begin to interact with others, develop and appreciate friendships and companionship, share toys, and make up games and rules in their play. This is the time to show him about taking turns and sharing.

Offer your child choice and let him explain how he came up with his decision. You can also add a different perspective to the scenario to broaden his vision and enhance his decision-making skills. Values and rules are passed on through daily activities, often without words.

It is helpful to give your child small tasks to do. This will give him a sense of responsibility, and teach him how to follow instructions, such as how to lay a table or water a plant or tidy up his toys. It will also give him an appreciation of the effort made by other people, such as mum's cooking or dad's lawn mowing, and help him consider others by keeping small toys away from his younger siblings. Children feel a great sense of achievement at completing a task, even it is done with your help. Offering him a star for his star-chart will make him proud. It works miracles at this stage.

Everything is subtly passed on through play, often without words, but through observations and mimicking how others interact with each other. He learns about the world through your filters. As he gets older, he will learn to make sense of everything and develop his own unique worldview. Your child learns best by acting out, imitating others and role-playing. Play also encourages independent thinking, decision-making, team working when he is older, and facilitates problem-solving skills and provides a healthy way to vent frustration and aggression.

Whether young or old, we all love to play deep down in our hearts and we don't do it regularly enough. As we grow older, we become too obsessed with the day-to-day running and do not to make time to have fun. Some of us might have even forgotten how to play. Having a child certainly makes you young again because you need to keep up the energy with him to entertain him when his friends are not around. So enjoy your time together now playing and having fun before he grows up all too quickly and disappears to school and his school friends.

Every child is a genius at something and your job is to find out what that is

I have come across very young authors or young traders who have naturally picked up their parents' hobbies and tried these out for themselves. This is by no means what will be their career when they grow up. But if they do love it and continue loving it, it's up to them to decide what they want to do when the time comes.

How to facilitate your child to learn?

Children develop and learn at different speeds. They also enjoy different things to play with at different stages. They learn through different sensory input channels, including watching, listening, touching, feeling, tasting, talking and acting out. Play comes in different shapes and forms, and stimulates all the different senses.

You will gradually notice as your child grows whether he is predominantly a visual learner who prefers looking or watching and finds it easy to utilise graphs, charts, maps and diagrams; an auditory learner who prefers to talk and listen as his way of information input; or a kinaesthetic learner who learns by doing.

We all use all our senses. However, most people have one or two dominant senses out of the five senses (sight, hearing, taste, smell and touch).

The last word

Devote time to play with your child, be present, and fully immerse yourself in his games. When mothers play, they tend to have other things on their mind for example, when to pick up their eldest from school and what's for supper. Play like a man who is totally present in that moment, forgets about his age when he plays with a child and behaves like a boy. Children love that.

Chapter 8

Potty Training

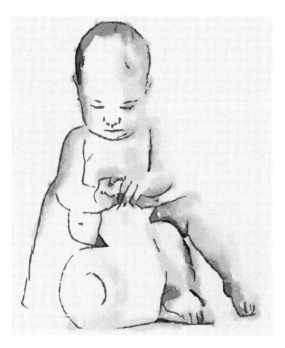

"Potty training is a developmental process, not a race!"

- Deedee & Dooley

Children normally become potty trained during the daytime between 18 and 36 months. If your child is not trained by the age of 3, I would encourage you to get further advice from a health visitor.

Most children are potty trained before they start nursery, although now there is no requirement for them to be trained before they start. Please let the carer/teacher know if he is not trained so that they can take him to the toilet or change his nappy regularly.

There isn't a set time for how long it should take to train a child to use a potty/toilet. It can take from a few days to a few weeks. It very much depends on the readiness of the child and the consistency of the parent.

Children who have a language delay or certain physical or mental conditions can still be potty trained, although they might take a little longer, and you might require more professional support and one-to-one advice.

Knowing when it's time

When your child is ready to be potty trained very much depends on his speech and language development, ability to follow simple commands and ability to control his bowel motions and bladder.

Wanting to have his nappy changed as soon as it's wet or soiled, being interested in talking about his pee or poop, or hiding in a corner when he is doing his business are clear signs of a child's readiness for potty training.

Getting started

Potty training requires consistency and patience, so the best time to start potty training is when you and your family are relaxed and enjoying your normal routine.

If you are distracted by other demands, for example, looking after a new baby, staying away from home on holiday or having visitors to stay, potty training can become frustrating for both you and your child.

Summer is obviously the easiest time to potty train your child, as you can allow him to run about in the garden without a nappy and it doesn't matter if he has an accident.

Pull-ups or normal undies?

Some parents prefer to put their child in pull-up nappies during potty training. Although easier to use, in my opinion, they are unnecessary (and costly) and possibly could prolong the training time, as the child doesn't feel the discomfort of being wet.

Potty or toddler toilet seat?

Some children prefer a potty; others prefer a toddler toilet seat, with a step up to the adult toilet.

Begin by introducing your child to the potty or toddler toilet seat and letting him get used to sitting on it without a nappy. You can make him feel comfortable by reading him a book, or telling him a story or singing a song while he is getting used to the potty/toilet.

Create a routine

Once you embark on the journey of potty training, you should be consistent with your practice in order to get your child there sooner and make your life easier.

By the age of 18 months, most children will have developed some kind of a routine. It is a good practice to sit your child on the potty or toilet first thing in the morning, last thing at night, before a bath and 15 to 30 minutes after he has had something to eat or drink. You can also ask him if he needs to use the potty/toilet regularly throughout the day. If using a potty, you should place it where it is easily seen and accessible by him.

Copying mummy and daddy

Children from 18 months onwards are curious about what you do and like to copy you. So you may find it helpful to encourage your child to sit on the potty when you are on the toilet or if your child is a boy when his dad is doing a wee standing.

Be encouraging

Potty training requires patience from you and lots of praise for your child, whether he has actually done a pee or poop in the potty/toilet, or has at least had a go by sitting on the potty/toilet for a few minutes.

Children love to see, hear or feel a reaction from you at this age. So make a big fuss or do a song and dance afterwards, which will feel like a huge reward for him.

By reacting to behaviour that you would like to see more of in the future, you will encourage your child to behave this way.

When you're out and about

You need to carry a potty with you wherever you go. This will give your child a clear message to about what he needs to do when he wants to pee or poop.

You also need to be ready when he is ready, however inconvenient. Whether that's halfway up the street or in a shopping centre, when he tells you he needs to go, you need to be ready.

If you are going out, give yourself plenty of time to prepare – suggest to your child that he uses the potty before you go out but take as much time as he requires. It is also good to plan your route so that you can stop somewhere convenient, and if possible private, if he needs to use the potty.

Accidents will happen

Accidents will happen, even once your child is potty trained. This can easily occur if he is not well or is feeling under the weather (for example, if he has just had an immunisation), when his routine is disrupted (for example, if you have visitors or are away on holiday), or if he is fully absorbed in playing or doing something and loses focus about his bodily needs.

Accidents can also happen when your child is in a new environment (such as his first day at nursery). He may be feeling nervous of using an unfamiliar toilet and too afraid to tell anyone that he needs to go.

If your child has an accident, you need to remain calm, cool and relaxed about it. Tell him that it is all okay and reassure him that accidents sometimes happen. Then simply change everything that needs changing.

Remember, children love your reaction. Any positive reaction is an incentive for him to want to see more by pleasing you. A negative reaction, such as you shouting, showing your disappointment or frustration, or getting upset, etc., will confuse and upset him, so it is critical that you remain calm.

If your child regresses, this could indicate that he has a urine infection, especially if his pee is smelly, or he has been vomiting with a temperature. He could be suffering from psychological distress such as starting nursery or being in a new place with new people and feeling anxious.

If your child is struggling

If your child is resisting your attempts to potty train him, you can give it a break for a week or two and try again at a later date. He will begin to use the potty when he is ready.

Holding on

Some children are uncomfortable at first using a potty or toilet, and may try to hold on to their poop, which can cause constipation.

It is not always clear why some children don't want to do a poop in the potty or toilet. It could be that the child was startled by a big splash when he previously pooped or his poop was hard and it hurt his bottom. Psychologists sometimes interpret this behaviour as attachment or reluctance to let something within them go.

From my clinical experience, poop training usually comes later, although research shows that most children can control their bowels before their bladder.

You can do your best to help your child by reassuring him and demonstrating that grown-ups also open their bowels. Having a little ceremony to say good-bye can help. You can also allow him to sit on the potty/toilet with a full nappy on, then gradually introduce a nappy with a hole cut out for poop to come out and then remove the nappy all together. It really is about whatever works for you and your child, so be creative. I would love to hear your stories to be used for any future editions of this book.

Night-time

Night-time potty training comes last and it can take up to the age of 6 for some children before they can go through the night without needing to pee or wake up to use the toilet.

When you begin to notice that your child's nappies are dry in the morning would be a good time for him to start sleeping in underpants, although there will be the odd accident at night.

You can go shopping with your child for their favourite undies, and praise them for being a big boy/girl, which can be a good incentive for your child to try to wake up if they need pee or poop during the night.

It is helpful to have a plastic sheet or mattress protector underneath the bed linen to keep the mattress clean.

Chapter 9

Ready for school

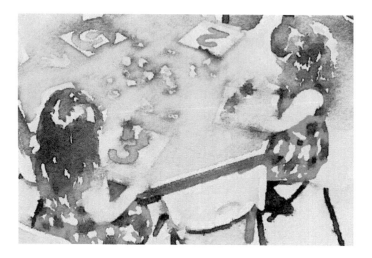

"Don't just teach your children to read... Teach them to question what they read. Teach them to question everything."

- George Carlin

Your child is now eating well, growing and meeting all his milestones. He is potty trained. You have his routine established perfectly so that he no longer naps, he sleeps through the night and he is able to get up early enough to be ready in time for his school run. Everything is on track now, right? There are just a couple of new concerns for parents.

Why children sometimes struggle to be in a social group in school

All parents seem to want their children to have friends, which apparently is at the top of their concerns, according to research. Based on what I have touched on the in Chapter 2 Love and Connection, the human needs psychologists consider that there are six fundamental needs driving our behaviour. We humans are social animals. We want to belong and yearn to be part of a group. It feels really unpleasant or painful if you are always outside a circle as I experienced in my childhood and youth for being the "odd one".

Your child may seem to be a bit shell-shocked because there are so many adjustments that he has to make, including a tighter routine, sitting down tasks and homework, especially if he was not so keen to start school. He also will meet new people in school, have to make new friends and do new activities. Since he has now started school, he will even be compared to other children of his age and be expected to compete against them.

You both might experience separation anxiety. He might even feel jealous about leaving you at home with his new sibling, or be concerned about you if you suffer from any form of physical or mental ill-health.

How to help him build his friendship group

Making friends is a skill. Like anything, the more you practise, the better at it you will be. You need to instil sufficient confidence for him to know that if one person or a group turns him down, there will be many others who will welcome him. This is simply a belief he could have in his mind that will help him along the way.

He could certainly do with your help to improve his social skills if he lacks the awareness or ability to interpret body language cues. Everyone knows that 93% of information is passed through non-verbal communication, such as body language and tone of voice, and only 7% of meaning is conveyed in words. Those children who do not understand these clues are hugely disadvantaged. You can help him learn to interpret cues and explain what these mean based on your observation, in order to help him to get it.

You could also help him by befriending the parents of his classmates by the school gate and inviting the children over to have little gatherings after school or at the weekend. Sometimes, people don't make an effort to get to know each other. You might feel so connected once you find out that you have so much in common after you start chatting with them because we tend to only connect with people who are like ourselves or who we are inspired to become.

Being connected in a social group is where you truly influence each other. Would you like your child's friends to try more fruit and salad? That's where you could treat them for tea at yours and give them a chance to practise healthy eating if that's not what they have at home. Those children might even go home and ask their parents to buy more fruit and salad. This is where we see the ripple effects in the community. You know deep down in your heart, this is what you want to see in a caring neighbourhood or society.

It might not be even your thing talking to other parents or inviting other children to your home, but if you knew this would give your child a head start in equipping him with adequate social skills and getting into a social group; would you do it for him?

He is growing independent of you as a parent

As your child becomes more independent, he will begin to utilise his analytical skills by making decisions on his own without looking into your eyes for any hint that you might have for him.

You have done a great job so far to instil your child with confidence, good habits, morals and beliefs so that he is able to achieve anything he wants. You perhaps have also tried to introduce him to different cultures, travel and meet new people to improve his social skills. That's excellent.

What you have programmed in him, by all means, sets an essential foundation for him. A very good one, albeit. However, the world is changing and everything is evolving. He is yet to have the whole life experience ahead of him to explore and venture. Wouldn't you want him to be able to test the water and dare to endeavour into the unknown and find out about the rest of the life himself even only in a relatively limited way at this stage?

How to encourage further confidence

Would you like your child to keep running on autopilot for the rest of his life from now on? Haven't you instilled the confidence in him to use his conscious mind to think and decide for himself? Wouldn't you want him to stand on his own feet to think for himself? You haven't brought him up to be a parrot who just repeats back what you say, to live in certainty without any attempt to explore the unknown. You trained him to be an active learner, question everything, which means that he is going to come home and confront you too one day. You have empowered him enough to express himself freely, to follow his heart and to feel worthy of enjoying life the way he wants it to be.

Devote time to talk to him quietly without disruptions each day. Be present, talk to him in a warm tone with good eye contact. Encourage a little discussion at home. Try to hear and understand the rationales behind his actions even if you don't approve of them. If you talk to him in a calm fashion, he will probably be more willing to tell you the truth. Consider some good questions that stimulate his thinking and help him look at things from different perspectives. This process will also help him see where you are coming from.

He now wants to try to decide for himself since this is the very first true physical separation in many children's lives. He might want to try something different, something he has not had before. After all, variety is another fundamental need that we all have as humans, plus children learn differently using visual, auditory and kinesthetic styles. For children who have a dominant kinesthetic learning style, they might prefer to learn about life by doing and experiencing. This includes making the inevitable mistakes themselves along the way, compared to those children who prefer to simply listen to their parents and accept things as truth.

There isn't a shortcut in our child' life journey. Sometimes as a parent, we think we can save our children from their pain and suffering. You can only do your best based on your knowledge and the parenting skills you have. He will need to find out the rest for himself.

If parents only criticise, this could lead to the child being rebellious and telling lies. An American psychologist claims that a child who grows up in a disciplined household being told about the rights and wrongs is just as likely to turn into a tearaway as those raised in chaotic homes, because he is out of your protective bubble and largely influenced by peers, his teachers, the education system and the rest of the environment that he is in.

Confidence can only be built in a nurturing home environment where learning and growth are facilitated and mistakes are tolerated. You must be able to have open communication based on love, trust, heartfelt understanding and acceptance for your child to feel safe and know that you are there for him no matter what. So it is not about never being able to make any mistakes in life, it is the knowledge that you are there to support him along the way.

Your role as parent for the rest of his journey

Life is all about balance. It's time to let go of some of the control. You can continue influencing your child absolutely if you remain his friend by listening to what he has to say and he has done in school. Only by doing so, you will be able to understand him and what drives his behaviour so that you know how to guide him. It is alright to have eaten a sweet or some processed food on the odd occasions such as at his friend's birthday party. Should you put all the focus on not eating sweets, he is more likely to have more. Please also refer to what I have discussed in Chapter 6 Love and Acceptance.

"Where focus goes, energy flows. "

- Wayne Dyer

Your role as a parent is not merely to programme your child to be what you want him to be, but to help him discover who he truly is. You are there to guide him, understand him when he disagrees with you and catch him when he falls. You can help him find his path in life; help him open all the doors to all possibilities.

Chapter 10

Self-Parenting

"If you truly loved yourself, you could never hurt another."

- Buddha

Everyone knows how we were brought up will have left a deep mark on how we think, feel and act, which in turn will affect how we parent. Each thought carries an emotion that directly impacts how we act or react to a situation.

This chapter is written especially for adults who did not or believe that they did not have the childhood they wanted or desired. Perhaps you felt something was missing or unjust, or in some cases, your parents were too preoccupied with their own interests or were simply busy working away from home.

I want to open your eyes to new possibilities and new techniques that could benefit you and your children's lives. With the awareness of new information, you can learn to parent consciously, knowing why you do certain things that you do. I am going to show you how you can give yourself that experience of a happy childhood when you want it.

In Chapter 2 Love and Connection, I touched on the six human needs and what we would do to meet those needs. We all need to have our needs met, whether we are the most selfless being or not. This is our animal instinct. Over the years, you have conditioned your body in certain ways, like having buttons on them, which when they are pushed, are guaranteed to make you react in certain ways because of neurons that fire together wire together.

Some things make you tick, while others are abhorrent to you. Most of these buttons were planted inside our bodies during our childhood by our parents and our environment, mostly subconsciously. The earlier they were in place, the stronger their effect. You might feel that you overreacted afterwards when you have calmed down. People tend to overreact when they are under stress, feel threatened, are losing control or feel powerless, and then become narrowly focused and selfish. Now you know why you did what you did and you can change it if you don't like it. It wasn't your fault up to this point because you were not aware of this.

In an ideal world, your parents would have understood about their own needs and how to meet them, so that they could have been happy and fulfilled beings who were totally devoted to your needs, and would have nurtured you and protected you with love from their hearts.

How many of us have experienced that kind of ideal parenting, because I don't believe it exists? I would love to hear from you if you had it. I would love to know how you are doing now and what was your journey like up to this point.

In reality, I hear many stories like mine, which was a quite uneventful, so-called normal childhood, being born into a performing arts family with both parents busy touring around China while I was looked after by half a dozen different nannies at different times.

I had few cherished memories apart from my "school lunch" which was served at a renowned Chinese restaurant called "MaKai", and those moments on my parents' return from their tours with lots of presents, which were probably their way for making up for their guilt at not being there for me, if you were to ask a psychologist. They were never around long enough either to offer encouragement or guidance so that I am the product of a truly free-range parenting style. For many decades, I actually struggled in silence, feeling alone, inadequate and melancholy, which I will describe in more detail in my upcoming autobiography "Life Begins at 50".

According to early attachment theory, Bowlby suggests that our recipe for an emotional bond with a primary carer is established in childhood. He gives importance to having one figure, the mother, the father or the nanny, for the child to attach himself to as a Safe Haven and who can act as a "Secure Base" in times of distress, during at least the first two years of his life.

A secure attachment helps regulate our autonomic nervous system so that our bodily functions become more organised and remain in homeostasis (a healthy state). In this state, we feel safe, confident, cooperative, caring, happy, creative, loved and connected, trusting, and we are able to express ourselves, balance our emotions, self-regulate and be stress-resilient. You can observe children who readily turn to their parents at times of distress and find comfort from their parents' reassurance. They feel safe to venture out and explore their environment because they know they can always return to their parents as a "Secure Base".

However, without secure attachment in childhood, trauma can result. Childhood trauma can result from various forms of child abuse to a minor surgery or any period of separation from the main carer. Each child is different and so is their stress-resilience and their threshold of mental or physical pain.

Sometimes trauma can occur even when the parent is physically around but without being truly present due to the lack of parental attunement. Some of the reasons for this lack of attunement could be due to parental substance misuse, depression, other mental or physical ill health, or special learning needs, and this can set their children's survival style (fight or flight response) in motion.

People with poor attachment tend to become more self-focused, vacant, suspicious, critical, rigid, impulsive, emotional, intolerant, anxious, fearful, disorganised, disorientated and retreat from goal-directed activities. These tendencies continue to impact their adult life, penetrating into all aspects of their lives, including school, college, job, home and relationships.

You can now sense the critical importance of having a secure attachment, but you may be wondering what you can do if you did not have one. There is hope.

Scientists have found an increasing amount of evidence that you can train your mind and change your brain. This is known as neuroplasticity. Results from scientific research have shown that the neurons (nerve cells) in the brain develop to compensate for injury and disease and to adjust their activities in response to new situations or changes in their environment. The brain apparently has the ability to rewire itself, making new connections in response to new information and experiences.

Neuroplasticity was originally believed to occur in children and remain unchanged throughout adulthood. However, this was found to be incorrect. Over the past 10 years, a number of studies have been carried out among patients with brain injuries. It was observed that there were micro changes to neurons and new neural networks resulting in remapping in healthy parts of the brain to restore some of the lost functions.

Your brain is changed by your experiences every day. Developing new habits or functions is like visiting a new place for the first time and you require satnav initially. It requires your intention and effort. If you keep doing it regularly, after a number of times, you can get there with little effort.

Once your brain is conditioned with the new information, it gets easier for your body to follow suit, do the things that it is being signalled to do. It becomes automatic in the end. You might be familiar with the saying "use it or lose it". If we continue learning, receiving new information, our brain will continue to develop new synaptic connections between neurons, while for unused connections, we lose them after some time.

Recent research on a group of nerve cells called "mirror neurones" shows that they fire regardless of whether you perform a task or observe a task. The potential implications of this have sparked huge interest among scientists. Can you recall a moment when you were feeding your child? You opened your mouth as the spoon approached his mouth. This is not usually a conscious behaviour. You had the intention in your mind of seeing your child opening his month and your body mirrored it so it opened as well. In return, your child mimics your opening his mouth for the spoonful of food when his mirror neurones are at work.

Here is another example. You were watching your home team playing on television. Your team won the match. Can you recall how that felt? You felt like you were on top of the world. You felt like a champion because that is true to your mind what you have perceived and believed. You scream for victory and tears run down your face because the brain does not distinguish whether it is you who is winning or the team you were watching. So why not create some mind movies to put yourself in that triumphant state of being. The mind leads and the body follows. If you do this, you can expect some real changes in your physical world.

Since the brain doesn't appear to distinguish whether it is a real experience or an imagined one, you can live the childhood you want, whenever you want, on demand, by creating your own mind movies, so that you can break the unwanted thought-feeling patterns and create new ones simply by thinking the wanted thought alone. The body knows how to generate the amazing feelings that automatically alter the biochemical changes in your body, and then comes the new expressions of your inner and outer world, including how you sit, walk, speak and behave in time.

Like the development of any habit, this requires regular practice. Treat yourself to this time alone with yourself. To start with, set 5-10 minutes aside daily to make peace with yourself and then increase the length of time as you progress. The more you practise, the easier it gets.

Practise through being mindful of your breathing or body sensations, what story or feelings come to mind, being present, compassionate and loving towards your young self. You know what you wanted from your parents and how you wanted it. Give it to yourself now. Hug yourself in the way you would love to have been hugged as a child, feel a pair of gentle arms around you or a big squeeze, and feel the warmth now. Feel that love now. What praise do you want to hear from your parents? Tell yourself now. With practice, you become empowered, nurtured, and feel protected and connected to yourself and others.

It must have been so heavy and exhausting to carry the baggage from the past, so now is a good time to drop this where it belongs – in the past. You are not your past. With regular practice, you will not rewrite your history, but you will transform your experience of that history. You will grow stronger in your mind, you will become emotionally more mature and you will assign events in the past with new meanings – from pain to growth, from failure to preparation, from learning to wisdom.

Your child and the people around you are also able to mimic what you do, possibly subconsciously, so be aware of your own state, what you are thinking and feeling. Check yourself in the mirror on the wall to make sure that your eyes are smiling, friendly, humorous, warm and welcoming, which will lead to your smiling lips and whole open body gesture.

Daily mindfulness exercise or meditation is beneficial for physical and mental well-being. Feeling the body, relaxing the body helps to develop a sense of here and now. It heightens the awareness of self and others so that you are more in tune and understand others' needs and your own needs better, and you are more in harmony with your environment.

There are other healing ways that you can experience. I have found that the process of writing this parenting book has not only provided information that benefits parents and parents to be but also has had a huge therapeutic power to my own wounds in my soul. I am hoping that it will help you in some way, whether you are a parent or not. You can identify an inspirational role model to develop a relationship with or get healed while nurturing others in a greater community.

The way that you have turned out to this point was not your fault without the information and awareness. But from now on, knowing that you have the power to control your mind for a new future, it will be your responsibility to end the past, end the blaming and leave the past in the past.

How to change your thoughts and feelings

We need emotions. Without them, we wouldn't bother to get out of bed or do anything. As humans, our behaviours are driven by our emotions. However, instead of being enslaved by our negative emotions, which are generated from a memory of a past event, we can master our emotions to feel the more elevated ones, such as happiness, joy, compassion and peace.

Why do some people seem to be happy all the time, while others are not? For them, being happy is a habit; it's what they focus their attention on.

Do you focus on the cup being half full or half empty? Our mind and body are intimately connected. What you think arouses how you feel, and becomes a learnt behaviour over the years that is wired in your brain and conditioned in your body by automatically altering your breathing, posture, the language patterns you use and even triggering a chain of biochemical changes in your body at different states. You can change your state of being by disrupting it anywhere in the chain of thought, feelings and behaviour. If you want to change, you simply need to break the mould and stop feeding that emotion you want to change.

It's like breaking an addiction. The parallel is that your emotion does alter your biochemistry in the body like any recreational drugs would do. It takes willpower, faith in your ability to carry through and belief that it's going to be worth it in the end.

You first need to learn to be aware of any negative thoughts or critical voice that feeds that negative emotion. Awareness of your state of being is the first step for change. You can easily stop your negative thoughts in their tracks once you are aware of them by simply altering your breathing, posture and internal self-talk. You can also change your behaviour by putting on your favourite music or run for five minutes or do something you love to change your mood and energy.

Negative emotion is a memory wired in the brain and felt in the body, in the same way as the happy emotions are. You might be able to recall some amazing memories when you listen to a piece of music or smell some nice cooking that reminds you of your childhood home. So make sure that you select your favourite music that lifts your mood.

There is a vast amount of evidence supporting the idea that exercise can help release the "happy hormones", including endorphins, dopamine and serotonin. Even if you feel resistance at the beginning, if you go out for a walk or run, you will always feel more alert and more focused afterwards. This gives you total satisfaction and joy with yourself after the exercise. So just give yourself a gentle push and set yourself a target of doing some regular exercise daily for 30 days. You are going to get used to it because this is how our nervous system works.

If you make a decision to react differently to how you would normally react to a situation, you are going to see a different result than what you would normally get. It's often not responding to a situation that pays the ultimate reward. Try it out. Experiment with it for maximum effect. It is quite a magical moment once you break that pattern. You know that you have done it and you can do it again in the future. Celebrate your victory.

If possible, try to avoid people or things that trigger your negative thoughts or emotions. One of the mothers, "E", who I visited suffered from post-natal depression with her first two children. Her mother suffered from depression all her life and had lived a separate life from her father. Although E had a great relationship with her father, she made a very tough decision not to see her mother much at all because she drained her. She subsequently reported feeling a sense of well-being during her current third pregnancy. She also reported an improved relationship with her husband and her two older children. I know very well that it is easier said than done sometimes to avoid people who affect us negatively, due to the different cultural influences and moral values that we have.

As I mentioned earlier, a song could trigger some sad feelings such as you had at the time when you broke up with your childhood sweetheart. If that is the case, you must delete that soundtrack from your album if you want to feel happy again. Reflect daily on how far you have come and cherish the wisdom you gained from the past. You deserve a second chance to be truly happy and fulfilled. Give it to yourself.

By now, you are developing new thought and feeling patterns that are more beneficial for your future self. But there is another layer of self that you need to be aware of – your value-belief system (critical factor filter), which is largely influenced by your upbringing. You and your partner probably have different value-belief systems, particularly if you are from different cultural backgrounds.

Your brain only allows information through the filter when it fits your value-belief system, by its ability to generalise, delete and distort information. We are all inundated with information throughout the day, with over 400 billion bits of information per second being processed via our five senses, so that the brain needs to make some executive decisions to make sense of the world quickly. So what appears to be truthful for you may not be for someone else with a different perspective.

As a conscious human being, we have the ability to recognise our thought patterns, negative traits or dysfunctional conflicts. Once we become aware of such, we are able to choose what we want to achieve and where we want to go, and decide by making a choice and taking actions towards a constructive and productive outcome.

Knowing what we now know, we can train our brain to be more kind, loving, nurturing, supporting and encouraging towards our inner child. We can heal our wounds if we choose to. You are one decision away from living a happy life and making everyone around you happy.

Afterword

"I cannot teach anybody anything; I can only make them think."

*- **Socrates***

The idea of writing a parenting book was born many years ago. Lots of the information that I've shared with people over the years has largely been the result of having the same conversation with the parents with little variation. I always thought parents knew what I was going to tell them and they surprised me every time when they didn't, including those parents from a medical background. Certainly, it has given me increased confidence by repetitively talking about the same thing over the years.

I actually started writing some of the chapters about two years ago. However, I didn't put enough focus on it and got distracted. I'm glad that I did. Over the past two years, I have completed some of the most intensive personal development training with Tony Robbins, Dr Joe Dispenza, William Whitecloud, Ryan Pinnick and

Anna Garcia. As a result, I have picked up enough courage to complete my very first book, *The Mother's Manual.*

The Mother's Manual was originally designed for parents, parents to be and want-to-be parents when I first started writing. However, as I was steadily making progress, I began to enjoy the immense therapeutic effect and healing power for myself by reading it and listening to it.

That's how the Self-Parenting chapter was born. I also decided to rewrite some of the chapters to incorporate the new knowledge and skills that I have gained in recent years as part of my personal journey.

We are all emotional beings. Our behaviour is affected each moment by our state of being. We need to be happy in order to see happiness around us. I have put a significant amount of emphasis on this in Chapter two: Love and Connection.

We also sometimes idealise situations, events or relationships, and easily fall into the trap of fault picking and complaining. We tend to think if only he did this or she had done that, I would be fine. The truth is that you are the only person who can give yourself anything you need. You would only be truly happy if all is coming from within. This includes a perfect childhood that you are indebted to.

Whatever the circumstances, knowing what we now know, we can heal ourselves. It might take time. At least, we can decide to choose the process of healing. We are not forgiving our parents for their sake only, but we are also doing this for ourselves to alleviate that pain trapped in the body. This will, in turn, make us healthier people and better parents.

I believe by reading some of the chapters in this book, people who may not have had decent parenting themselves, whether they are parents or not, may be able to find some comfort. What happened in their lives or their parents' lives when they were little was not their fault. They will understand that there is nothing wrong with them and, more importantly, learn what they can do now to help themselves be happier people and happier parents.

I want to conclude that nobody is perfect. We are all human at the end of the day. However, all you need to know is that there is nothing more important than the present moment, so do what you know best with the purest love and intentions to move forward. You cannot change the past or whatever mistakes you made, but you can make a huge impact on the future of yourself and your children if you parent consciously now. Be aware what you say, do and hear, and be aware what kind of human being you want to create, be clear where you want to take your child; the words will come out just right from your mouth.

All we can do is to continuously try our best based on what we know and move forward toward the outcomes that we want. This is an individual journey. Everyone progresses according to her level of awareness. It is an incredible feeling, making progress towards your goal regardless how small those steps are.

Knowing what you know now, with the powerful mind, you can give yourself the most amazing childhood that you desired! There is no time or space between the past or future; there is no difference between imagination and reality in our mind's eye. So, how would you like your childhood to be? Run that movie in your mind again and again. Feel how you would feel, hear what you would hear, imagine the love, smile, nurture, support and encouragement you crave. It is never too late to have that perfect childhood.

I thank you for reading the book to the end. I hope that you have enjoyed it and find something useful or whatever you were searching for. Please share it with others who might find that this handy little book is all that they need to spark their awakening. Spread the words of a good read. With all my best wishes and gratitude to you.

Join *The Mother's Manual* community

Welcome on board of ***The Mother's Manual*** Community. May Young Lilies nurture you and let's nurture each other together. I invite you to experiment with everything you've learnt from the book, observe the results – knowledge is only information until you make use of it – take action consistently and make small changes towards achieving your desired outcomes continuously.

There are lots the food for thought. I very much hope that I have opened some doors or shone some light on your path and sparked sufficient interest for you to embark on the journey of self-discovery. I urge you not to accept all the information in this book as gospel truth.

I appreciate your comments if you could share them with me via

www.YoungLilies.com

Email *Lil@YoungLilies.com*

Facebook group *#TheMother'sManual*

Skype *The Mother's Manual* group link

https://join.skype.com/aUoQc86rjagW

Appendix 1
Understanding your child

"Rebellion is a sign of a child fighting to be seen as who they are."

- Carol Tuttle

We are all different. By now you know your child's character. Some are quiet and happy to sit down and read, while others enjoy outdoor activities more. As a parent, your role is to understand your children, accept them for who they are, guide and encourage them to explore their path called life, to most effectively develop what they are lacking and further strengthen what they are good at.

You can encourage a sedentary child doing some outdoor activities and plan for some quiet reading time if he is a wild child. The rule of thumb is to start on an activity that is his least favourite for about 5-10 minutes at a time. You can build on that should you wish to gradually. Keep doing those activities on a regular basis until his body is used to it.

Nine types of personality

The **Enneagram of Personality** comes from the Greek words έννέα γράμμα meaning nine types, although it is unclear to exactly who wrote them down. They are Helper, Achiever, Loving Soul, Thinker, Sceptic, Adventurer, Leader, Peacemaker and Perfectionist.

This ancient personality system is still very much relevant and alive today and has been further developed by many modern psychologists and psychiatrists. The basics of the Enneagram give us some insight to understand who we are and what's driving our behaviour; furthermore, it helps us to understand our children and what's the best way to guide and nurture them.

We all appear to have a dominant aspect of our personality from one of the nine types, although our behaviours are also influenced by our environment, for example, whether it is calm and productive, or stressful and aggravating. Furthermore, our personalities are also influenced by our neighbouring types like in astrology, for instance, whether you are on the Sagittarius-Capricorn cusp if your birthday falls during the transition period.

The nine types of personalities are divided into three subtypes based on our typical behavioural patterns, which originate from our innate autonomic nervous responses, known as the fight-or-flight response, a hyperarousal state towards a perceived threat to survival. If the threat is so intense, it triggers the freeze behaviour/feigning death such as seen by a deer when chased by a predator getting too close.

However, the part of the brain responding to the threat, the amygdala, does not distinguish between a real threat or an imagined one. Subsequently, it triggers the hypothalamus, pituitary gland and adrenal cortex to secrete various chemical messengers and hormones like cortisol and adrenaline, which increase heart rate, blood pressure, blood sugar, tunnel vision, tremors, dry mouth, dilated pupils, relaxed bladder, slowed digestion and suppressed immune responses. This response gives the body a boost of energy to focus on dealing with what is in front that is perceived as an imminent danger.

We can turn on our defensive mechanism if we simply think or feel we are under attack. Our body can manage in this survival mode for a short-term; however, long-term survival states such as chronic stress can cause disease in our body.

The Helper, Achiever and Loving Soul are feeling, heart-centred people with the innate flight response. They have a tendency to abandon the body, not feeling the body and its needs. They have a melancholy tendency. The Helper avoids such feelings by creating a likeable image by looking after other people. Achievers try to avoid their feelings by throwing themselves into their studies in order to receive positive feedback and affirmation from others. The Loving Soul escapes her negative feelings by creating a sense of her unique self.

The Thinker, Sceptic and Adventurer are logical, head-centred people who have a tendency to react to fear with the freeze response. The thinker deals with fear by retreating into his mind. The Sceptic deals with fear by preparing for the worst scenarios and trying to avoid them. The Adventurer deals with fear by turning an uncomfortable body experience into excitement to metabolise fear.

The Leader, Peacemaker and Perfectionist are instinctive, body-centred people who have a tendency towards anger with the fight response. Leaders act out their anger and express it easily, while Peacemakers are most out of touch with this emotion and disconnect from anger, instead, portraying a harmonious persona. Perfectionists internalise their anger and are very critical of themselves and others.

This is only a guide for the most common character types, known as stereotypes. Personality is fluid in nature. There are so many factors that can influence your child's personality. For instance, he might behave differently when he is in a relaxed environment compared to when he is feeling anxious in a stressful environment.

Aisha is a little Helper. She is quite popular with children, teachers and parents. She wants to please everyone. She likes to be needed. She can be sensitive to disapproval and criticism. She sometimes feels that her needs are being overlooked by others and this can lead to feelings of rejection. Over time, to avoid the pain, she gradually loses sight of her own needs and instead focuses on everyone else's, which is how she gets most joy.

Best parenting style for a little Helper is to tell her that she is very much loved and appreciated for her help and consideration. Share fun times with her. Take an interest in her problems or needs. Ask her how *she* feels and whether *she* needs help. Offer support. Be gentle if you need to correct her.

Christopher is a little Achiever. He works hard and is top of everything in the nursery. He is well liked by other children and adults. He set goals, such as going to the top university from as young as the age of 3, like his big brother and dad doing a successful job. He fears that nobody will love him if he doesn't achieve top grades.

Best parenting style for little Achiever is to help him to achieve his best by providing a harmonious and peaceful environment, and leaving him alone when he is doing his work. Tell him how proud you are of all his effort and be there for all his disappointments because he thought you would only love him if he achieved the top grade. This is the time for you to help him build resilience and develop humility. It's important to demonstrate your unconditional love in the time of need to show him that you love him for who he is and however he is. Remind him to have some fun some time to keep a good balance in life.

Mini is truly a Loving Soul. She has an active imagination and is happy to play alone with her imaginary friends. She can be seen as a loner sometimes and doesn't always like playing with the other children. She only attaches herself to an idealised version of teachers, role models, stars, etc. She can become rebellious when being criticised or misunderstood, even though she very much wants people to understand her. This can really spiral into a melodrama.

Best parenting style for a Loving Soul. She has a need to be special. She likes to be offered plenty of sincere compliments. Respect her gift of sensitivity and depth in her thoughts by being a good listener and friend. Accept her sensitivity. Understand her by asking questions with sincerity and tentativeness, demonstrate with words and actions that she has your complete wholehearted acceptance and give her time to be with herself when necessary.

Alexander is a little Thinker. He spends a lot of time alone reading, learning, playing computer games or making collections. He has few friends, although he is very bright and makes good grades; however, girls just cannot crack the nut and get close. He appears to be a grown-up with an independent mind. He often has sharp questions for his parents and teachers. He talks little but absorbs every single piece of information he receives. He may find the social demands of school challenging.

Best parenting style for a little Thinker is to allow him to be independent and give him time to be alone to process his feelings and thoughts. He doesn't share what's on his mind with you because he finds it difficult to share his thoughts and feelings. Offer supportive tentatively. You may want to excuse him from attending his classmates' parties if he doesn't want to go.

Jonty is a little Sceptic who often has a friendly, likeable outlook and can follow the rules but deep down he distrusts others and can sometimes come across as being bossy or stubborn. He wants to take care of all eventualities himself so that he won't be let down by anyone and so that he feels prepared if anything unexpected should happen. He can swing between being funny and being anxious or hyper-vigilant, looking out for signs of danger in his world. He can fly off the handle if things don't quite work out the way he planned.

Best parenting style for little Sceptic is to be direct and clear about what you expect of him using a gentle manner. Reassure him that everything is alright between you and that you love him unconditionally. Listen to him when he has something to share and laugh with him naturally whenever possible.

Marsha is an Adventurer. She loves outdoor thrills such as skateboarding or roller coasting and finds it difficult to sit still. She doesn't waste any energy dwelling on sorrows on her mind. Instead, she loves doing things that she can experience in her body and is always on the go. She dreams of freedom and is more content when being alone. She is naturally curious and inquisitive with a vivid imagination.

Best parenting style for the Adventurer is to support her in what she is doing and tell her that you care about her. The best reward for her is to engage her in stimulating conversation and laughter, show your affection to her and give her freedom.

Lara is a little Leader. She is independent and has an inner strength and a fighting spirit. She takes the lead and seizes control whenever possible and will attack verbally or physically when provoked. She has this protective armour around her and never wants to be controlled or show anyone that she has a soft spot.

Best parenting style for little Leader is to be direct with her, give her space to be alone, and acknowledge sincerely the contribution that she makes. Do not take it personally if she screams or stomps around; it's just the way she is. Sometimes, it is good for her to see your vulnerable side, which might lead to a neutral sharing of feelings.

Amir is a Peacemaker. He cannot bear to be in the middle of a conflict, so he tunes out a lot, especially when others argue. He is described by his parents and teachers as a good child because he never gets angry or throws a temper tantrum. He is easy-going and has a calming soothing effect on the people around him. However, he can display inward anger when the unhappiness builds up inside him, especially if he feels unjustly treated and thinks he is being overlooked.

Best parenting style for little Peacemaker is to listen to him intently when he is talking and give him time to make decisions. It is alright to nudge him gently especially if you want to utilise his popularity and companionable qualities to work with his peers in a group. Remember to praise him for giving him lots of physical contact to show your affection.

Anna is a Perfectionist. She can really give herself and others a hard time for breaking the rules or for doing a job poorly. Her inner critic will not accept anything but perfection, which is hard to achieve. She does not allow for any mistakes. She is very responsible and may grow up too fast to resume the role of the parent. She can also be competitive by comparing notes with others and asking lots of questions in order to be at the top of the class.

Best parenting style for the Perfectionist is to take some of the responsibilities off her if you think she has taken on too much. Acknowledge her achievements and reassure her that she is great as she is. Tell her that you value her advice and apologise if you have been thoughtless.

In general, regardless of your child's character or personality, as a parent, you need to accept them for who they are and respect them, as you would do to an adult person. Try to get into their world and see things from their perspective. Be available to them and there when they need you. Acknowledge their presence, and praise their efforts, contributions and achievements whenever possible. Tell them how much you love them.

Demonstrate what you would like them to do if they are misbehaving. Offer them hugs and kisses and give them time alone if required also. By gently leading them into doing the activities they may not naturally gravitate to, you can help them develop new skills, new muscles in the brain, build their confidence, and broaden their experience.

Appendix 2 Meditation—

Having a Happy Childhood

"It's never too late to have a happy childhood."

- Tony Robbins

In this section, I explain how you can meditate on "Having a Happy Childhood" in order to experience the love and acceptance you may have missed out on in childhood.

If you would like to listen to a full, guided meditation on "Having a Happy Childhood", you can download it for free from the Young Lilies website: www.YoungLilies.com

As I explain in Chapter 10 Self-Parenting, the brain does not distinguish between a true external experience and an internal experience that is purely generated by your mind. Therefore, you can generate elevated emotions (such as love, joy, happiness, peace), regardless of your current situation. Doing so will produce a chain of biochemical changes that are real to your body.

We all have some happy childhood memories, big or small. Your conscious mind might not remember it, but your subconscious mind memorises all deep down. You can only access this information when you are very relaxed. By accessing the power of your subconscious mind, you can experience a happy childhood whenever you want to on demand.

If you can't recall a happy memory, then you can use your imagination to create one. Be a scriptwriter, a film director and the principal actor all in one. Put yourself in the role of maybe a childhood friend whose parents treated him in the way you wish your parents had treated you. You can give yourself that experience now.

Read the instructions below first and when you are ready to begin, set aside about 15 minutes. Find a quiet space without any disruptions. Turn off your mobile phone. Drink plenty of water before and after this mental exercise.

Take a couple of deep breaths and close your eyes. Let all the external sounds diminish into the background.

This time is just for you.
Imagine a wave of relaxation flowing down from the very top of your head, like a warm shower, pouring down your face, neck and your whole body.

Relax your forehead and smooth out all the creases, relax the tiny muscles around your eyes and jaw, relax your tongue, let your jaw hang lose with your lips slightly open; relax your shoulders and arms all the way through to your fingertips; relax your legs all the way to your toes and the soles of your feet.
...

Remember a time or imagine a situation that brings you happiness, love, joy, peace. Bring a big grin on your face now. That's right. Allow all the happy hormones to flow freely through your body now, triggering those wonderful feelings in your body.
...

Now all the external sounds are coming back. You may open your eyes when you are ready with that big grin on your face. Stay in that place until you feel energetic and upbeat to return to your daily life with those elevated emotions.

You have just exercised the power of the subconscious mind. You now know how you can experience a happy childhood whenever you want to on demand. Give yourself those wonderful feelings that you deserve on a regular basis. You are the only person who can make you happy. Enjoy life!

About the Author

Liu Yang

BSc MSc MCNHC FRSPH

Health Visitor practice teacher

Hypnotherapist / Life Coach

After working with children and families for over 20 years and extensive personal development training, Liu Yang brings you the best of her knowledge and expertise to help you understand yourself, your emotions, needs, thoughts and relationships, and how these relate to your life as a parent.

This book provides everything you need through simple strategies to help raise a happy child, realise their full potential and enable you to be a proud, well-balanced and fulfilled parent.

Being a fellow of the Royal Society for Public Health, Liu has focused her work on improving people's mental well-being by working with children and parents. Find out more about Liu and the programmes she offers on

www.YoungLilies.com

or email

Lil@YoungLilies.com

May you find this book helpful in some way

Note

Our sincere thank goes to

Laura Ehlis
Liz Peak
Rahima Khan
Julia Billington
Shay Malone
Nadia Dubiel
Sonia Sofka
Ilona Redfern

The author has rewritten some of the chapters to accommodate their ideas and questions. Also our sincere thank goes to those who liked, shared and supported the posts at The Mother's Manual launch team. They are:

Anna Garcia
Louise Kennedy
Steve Oakley
Shanthini Shanmugaguru
Laura Helen Herbert
Susan Gault
Christine Bradly
Suzi Dickinson
Pravina Patel
Jean Godfrey
Jasmin Hearts
Jag Kumari
Juline Bruck
Er Aiyaz Quadri
Jean Marc Koffi
Sarah Louise Hunter Carson
Anand Dobalee Rai
Mariasol Ling Rouse
Tom Coy
Tracey Hussey
Michelle Lois Wilson

Mark Strefford
Atul Thakrat
Ananda Siu Ying
Feyi Ventures
Chukwudum Ikeazor
Milon Ahmed
Saw Min Oo
Em Zackaria Suzy
Kehide Olarin Moye
Paolo Mereu
Matthew Cybulski
Sandra G M Jarvis
Ayodele Daudn
Kehinde Olarinmye
Amini Bhakta
Chee Kong Yeung
Yan Chen
Erin O'Donnell
Juan Rivera
Suraj Maharjan

Notes